T0366245

IN THE
REARVIEW
MIRROR

In the
Rearview
Mirror

A perspective on a
selective collective of
reflexive reflectives
and **recollectives,**
sans invectives

By: Jerry W. "Slats" Jackson

authorHOUSE®

AuthorHouse™
1663 Liberty Drive
Bloomington, IN 47403
www.authorhouse.com
Phone: 1-800-839-8640

© 2011 Jerry W. "Slats" Jackson. All rights reserved.

No part of this book may be reproduced, stored in a retrieval system, or transmitted by any means without the written permission of the author.

First published by AuthorHouse   10/03/2011

ISBN: 978-1-4634-6824-8 (sc)
ISBN: 978-1-4634-6822-4(ebk)

Library of Congress Control Number: 2011915114

Printed in the United States of America

Any people depicted in stock imagery provided by Thinkstock are models, and such images are being used for illustrative purposes only. Certain stock imagery © Thinkstock.

This book is printed on acid-free paper.

Because of the dynamic nature of the Internet, any web addresses or links contained in this book may have changed since publication and may no longer be valid. The views expressed in this work are solely those of the author and do not necessarily reflect the views of the publisher, and the publisher hereby disclaims any responsibility for them.

Dedicated to my wife Pat,
who has been my "right hand"
in putting this batch of columns together
while putting up with my eccentricities for 50 years
and to our children—son Kerry and daughter Shannon—
both of whom are armed with goodness and compassion.

TABLE OF CONTENTS

FOREWORD

Actually, the only hint of plagiarism to be found in this book is in the title. But it's not *pure* plagiarism because it doesn't mention Lubbock title-wise, although it very well could.

If you're not familiar with the song, here's the ending in the immortal lyrics of Mac Davis:

I guess happiness was Lubbock, Texas
In my rearview mirror
But now happiness is Lubbock, Texas
Growing nearer and dearer

And the vision is getting clearer
In my dreams
And I think I finally know
Just what it means
And when I die you can bury me
In Lubbock, Texas, in my jeans

Thank you, Google, for those heartfelt words, along with the noticeable lack of punctuation. And Mac, wherever you are, please don't sue me for infringement because I look on you as a "good old boy" from Lubbock, and am confident that you probably won't come down on a "so-so old boy" who is also from there. Also, though we've never met, Lubbock remains close to both our hearts. After all, I was born there in the family home on Avenue H, which has since been re-tagged as Buddy Holly Avenue. How many other people can boast that they were born on that rechristened street? Precious few, if any, I would imagine.

Yeah, our old hometown hangs heavy in many of my ramblings in this book. It was home to me from the time I "discovered America" back in 1932 until I was inducted into Uncle Sam's Army after graduating from Texas Tech in 1955. Incidentally, those two years in the military were enjoyable ones. We had just quit shooting in Korea and hadn't resumed the practice until Vietnam. I lucked out by landing at Fort Ord, Calif., for basic training. Nice spot for that duty, just a stone's throw from such exotic places as Pebble Beach and Cannery Row. (Actually, I wasn't much of a gung ho soldier. I was lousy on the firing range, where "Maggie's drawers"–a euphemism for that white flag that another soldier waved when one's bullet missed not only the bull's-eye but the *entire target*–was commonplace in my case. But what you must understand is that the only other gun I had fired previously was a weapon of minimal destruction–a Red Ryder BB gun–so what could you expect?) So they figured that I was a good candidate for clerk-typist school and sent me, following boot camp, to 5th Army Headquarters in Chicago at 51st and Hyde Park streets–hard by Lake Michigan–where I typed up reenlistment assignments to my heart's content before talking up to my CWO boss that I really, really would like to do my typing in

Germany. So he had this friend, CWO Emerick, with the 8th Infantry Division Headquarters at Fort Carson in Colorado Springs, who he said would soon be "gyroscoping to Germany" (that would make a great song title, eh?) and he prevailed on him to take me in. So I spent that summer of '56 (a good season to be there) at Carson before switching places with the division in Germany, my promised land that was full of joy and contentment.

But enough blathering about the Army so as to move along to some background on other goings and doings. I lived in two other houses in addition to the one in which I was born until age 6, when my parents built our home at 20th and R streets in Lubbock. I lived there while attending Dupre Elementary, junior high, Lubbock High and Tech, which served as nice roots for me. My parents? Simply super, along with my brother Gene and sister Shirley. After returning from the Army (from which I received only one medal–the Good Conduct Medal for not doing anything really bad–it came with a red and white ribbon, as I recall), I gravitated to Snyder, 90 or so miles southeast of Lubbock, where I figured production of gasoline, butane and propane at the Lion Oil Co. plant for a couple of years before falling into newspapering. You see, the Snyder Daily News lost its sports editor to a more lucrative sports editing job in Corpus Christi, so I responded despite never having had any journalism training. No problem, though, because I think they were only looking for someone who could just put a sentence together and I qualified on that score.

I was with the Daily News in that capacity for several years, and it was during that span that I lucked out and met Patricia Shilcutt, with whom I eventually "tied the knot" in 1961. Now, it would be fair for you to wonder how I happened to meet Pat, as I was toiling in Snyder and she was a student at Tech. It was on a blind date arranged by one of my two roommates, Dub Holt, who was also a Tech grad and was dating Pat's dorm roomie, Jan Preston, at the time. So it was that the four of us got together for a Tech-Houston football game at the Clifford B. & Audrey Jones Stadium there in Lubbock (fortunately, the name has since been mercifully shortened). Anecdotally, Pat mentioned to us that she had once before seen Tech and Houston go at it on the gridiron, and recalled that it was a low-scoring contest. "I think it was 1-0," she said. Well, Dub and I got our jollies out of that comment, since that's the only score it *couldn't* have been. It could've been 0-0, 2-0, 3-0, etc., but it's not possible to score an extra point without getting a touchdown first. Dub lives in Waco now, but anytime we see each other or talk on the phone, we tend to look back on Pat's stated low score and sort of guffaw.

Speaking of Dub, who was working as a speech therapist in the public school system there in Snyder, I'd like to point out our living arrangements. We paid rent to a fellow named Wayne Whitaker, who owned the house in which the three of us resided. Now, Wayne was a very ambitious guy who, in addition to a full-time job as an engineer for Chevron, also was in the habit of buying other houses, fixing them up and selling them at a profit. And it paid off for him handsomely. Dub and I, on the other hand, evinced more of a laid-backness, preferring to improve our minds by watching the Three Stooges and Amos 'n' Andy on TV whenever possible. It made for an enjoyable existence, but was sort of fiscally irresponsible. Oh, well . . .

Meanwhile, Pat and I went on to produce two great kids who turned out right–son Kerry, born in 1963, and daughter Shannon, who came along five years later. We've had a good life. No complaints there.

To capsulize my work history, Pat, Kerry and I relocated from Snyder to Brownfield, Texas, in 1963, where I worked as editor of the *Brownfield News-Herald* for two years before moving on to Prescott, Ariz., where I started out as a general assignments reporter at the then *Prescott Evening Courier* and ended up as managing editor before moving to California and a 27-year tenure with the *Sacramento Bee.* (As an aside, my all-time favorite editors to work under were Jim Garner at the *Courier* and Frank McCulloch at the *Bee.*) Following retirement from the *Bee* in 1995, we returned to Prescott, where I worked as a reporter and copy editor until re-retiring in 2005. I continue to write a weekly column–700-plus of the things since returning to Prescott–while remaining active in the Prescott Noon Lions Club and singing in two choirs and warbling in a men's trio at the Prescott United Methodist Church. Life, as noted *ad nauseam,* is good.

Now, regarding that silly subtitle on the cover. I must admit that "recollectives" isn't even a legitimate word, but I just like the sound of it along with those other words ending in ive(s). But rest assured that the inclusion of "sans invectives" is sincere, as the columns are G-rated. So it's OK if you'd like to let the kids read 'em if they're interested and there's nothing much on TV at the time or they get bored with Facebook and Twittering. There's absolutely no plot to follow, so it makes for mindless reading. Punditry, not profundity, predominates.

And, oh . . . in the immortal words of the late Peter Falk: "One other thing . . ." A high school buddy, Earl Dietering, hung that "Slats" nickname on me after becoming aware of one Martin "Slats" Marion, a shortstop with the St. Louis Cardinals during the 1940s. According to Google, Marion "had unusually long arms, which reached for grounders like tentacles, prompting sportswriters to call him 'The Octopus'." So they settled on labeling him as "Slats" because "Octopus" reached too far and had too many syllables for most headlines. Anyway, Earl noticed that I had long arms too (actually, they reach all the way to my fingertips) and figured that "Slats" fit nicely based on my slight frame and, I suspect, that Jerry "Octopus" Jackson tended to sound ridiculous.

—Jerry "Slats" Jackson

I'M HERE TO TELL THAT I DIDN'T SPELL WELL

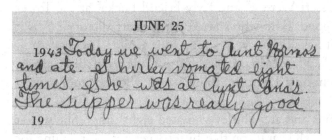

JUNE 25

1943 Today we went to Aunt Norna's and ate. Shirley vomated eight times. She was at Aunt Cana's. The supper was really good

19

Diary Entry

What you must understand, going in, is that I was only 10 years old at the time and my sophistication, and spelling, clearly reflected that.

The year was 1943, and I kept a diary–diligently–from early February to late July before pooping out.

Here are some excerpts, followed by contemporary parenthetical pronouncements. And please forgive the various silly spellings, which range from the phonetic to the pathetic. Here goes:

Feb. 6–I have a sour sworth and it really hurts. (I *think* I was trying to say "sore throat," but, in my abject misery, was talking sort of funny.)

Feb. 11–This evening I played baseball out on the field. It was a pretty day. Tonight I got a whipping about the dishes. (Those dirty, good-for-nothin' dishes!)

Feb, 14–Today was valatines day and I have 18 valatines so far. (They loved me when I was a kid.)

Feb. 16–Tonight I listened to "Fibber Megee and Molly," "Bob Hope," and Red Skelton. I had just got in town at school and the bell rang. (Why was Bob in quotation marks and Red wasn't? Was that really Hope on the radio or someone posturing for him? We'll never know.)

Feb. 27–Tonight Mother went to town and got me, Shirley and Sandra a pop and hotgod. (I can almost taste that hotgod *right now!*)

March 4–Floyd, Charles, Bill and I played Monply for about 4 minutes. (Hey, guys, that's not even enough time to get to Boardwalk and/or Park Place. And let's try doing a better job on spelling Monopoly, huh?)

March 5–Today Nancy Ketron was moved from me and now she sits by Ross Craig. Today I had a real bad stomock acke. It felt like rocks rolling around. (Ah, yes, Nancy Ketron . . . the most luscious morsel in the whole 5th grade at Dupre Elementary back there in Lubbock, and a person with whom both Ross and I were hopelessly in love. "Hopelessly" is the key word here, because her relationship with both of us was perfectly platonic, to say nothing of unrequited. Woe was we. Or "us," as the case may be.)

1

By: Jerry W. "Slats" Jackson

April 1–Today is April fool's and I fooled Bill four times on the way to school. (Bill always was a slow learner.)

April 12–Today Patsy's daddy gave a free pass to Patsy and Patsy gave the pass to the Arcadia to Shirley and she gave it to me. (Well, that's *that.*)

April 20–Today is Hitler's birthday. He is 54 today. This evening I got two grand slams, 1 tootie roll and 3 choclate bars. I played marbles with Bill. (Happy birthday to you, happy birthday to you, happy *birth*day, dear Adolf, happy birthday to you!)

May 7–This evening I went to see "Dessert Victory" and "My Friend Flicka" at the Tower with Bill, mother and daddy. It was pretty good. (Uh, who starred in "Dessert Victory"? Was it James Mason? George C. Scott? Or could it have been a very young Julia Child?)

May 15–I went to see "The Apache Kid," "Murder in the Big House," "Lightnin' Bill Carson" and "Blondie For Victory." I liked all of them but "Lightnin' Bill Carson." (Sounds to me like a classic case of overkill.)

June 25–Today we went to Aunt Norma's and ate. Shirley vomated eight times. She was at Aunt Edna's. The supper was really good. (I'll call it quits on that bittersweet note. One thing for sure, though, I really am glad that I was over at Aunt Norma's that day!)

Prescott Courier, January 1998

'TIS THE SEASON FOR MEMORIES FROM A WEST TEXAS CHILDHOOD

So Harry had his flying red horse, but we had our greasy brown cow. Had the two animals mated, there's no telling what sort of creature might've evolved.

The question from the lady in the church office awhile back was a searching one: "Are you going to write something for this year's Advent devotional booklet?" I hadn't thought about it until that Tuesday, and the deadline for submissions, she said, was two days away. Well, I tend to be more emotional than devotional, being a person incapable of serious thinking, so I decided to tell about how I got skinny one Christmas as a post-toddler while living in Grandma's house.

Now, what you must understand from the outset is that I chronicle my early years according to events that took place in the three houses in which I lived from birth to age 6, leading up to Sept. 1, 1939, when my family moved into the house at 20th Street and Avenue R in Lubbock, Texas, where I resided from first grade through college. (I remember the date because it was on that very day that Hitler unleashed his Stukas on Warsaw, dive-bombing the city and kicking off World War II in earnest.) The three-bedroomer was new, cost $4,500 for house and lot, and the monthly mortgage payment was $39. We were in the midst of the Depression, as many of you may recall, and that $39 represented about one-quarter of my dad's salary, so things haven't changed all that much percentage-wise.

The first house I lived in was the one in which I was born–on Avenue H about a mile from downtown Lubbock–and I remember it well, although I couldn't have been more than 2 years old when my family moved to Grandma's house. (We called it that because, well, my paternal grandmother owned it. Not too terribly imaginative, but very factual.) Even at that tender age, though, I have memories of that place on Avenue H, such as my mother and a couple of aunts snapping black-eyed peas in the back yard (my brother Gene, who was eight years older than me, called them blue-eyed beans–possibly as a joke, but we'll never know), and the time when our cow fell into the grease pit at Harry Hazel's Mobil station across the street. I have no idea how she managed to get loose and stray over there, but it took several men to hoist her out. So Harry had his flying red horse, but we had our greasy brown cow. Had the two animals mated, there's no telling what sort of creature might've evolved.

But getting back to Grandma's house and the strange point of this epistle. You see, I was a typically tubby toddler when the family moved there, but leading up to Christmas that year–when I was on the brink of my third or fourth birthday, I forget which–I contracted an industrial-strength case of whooping cough, which brought on a state of skinniness. And the condition has held on pretty much so that now, in my twilight years, I'm still relatively skinny except for a cute little potbelly. As an aside, when Uncle Sam inducted me into the Army in

By: Jerry W. "Slats" Jackson

1955, the Military Manual of What's Permissible and What Ain't (that's not the formal title, but close enough) stated that to be eligible for service a person of my height (6-4 and a half) must weigh at least 160 pounds, but I was a scrawny 155. Not to worry, though. "Aw, we'll fatten you up," the sergeant on duty assured me, then added, "please step off the scale so we can swear you in," or words to that effect. And sure enough, that good old Army chow, coupled with regular hours and exercise, resulted in my gaining 10 pounds during the 16 weeks of basic training and I ballooned into an absolute butterball, relatively speaking.

But I seem to have strayed from that memorable Christmas at Grandma's house. That was the one when Santa, bless his beefy bones, presented me with an electric train, and the memory of that Christmas morning and hoped-for gift are as vivid today as if it were yesterday. The set featured a little depot and had cargo that included logs and oil drums that I immediately became adept at loading and unloading into and out of the boxcars, and both Mom and Dad marveled at my unpracticed expertise. (I really hate to brag in that regard, but there's an old saying that "he who tooteth not his own horn, the same shall remain untooted." I'm not sure who wrote those cogent words, but it sounds a lot like Shakespeare.)

Hey, I've exceeded my allotted space and haven't even touched on the *third* house I lived in before settling in on that long stretch on Avenue R. It was a rental place on Avenue J, a few blocks from downtown, that we dubbed "the Carlock house" because a Mr. Carlock was the owner. (Like "Grandma's house," the designation isn't too inventive, but embodies a certain practicality.) I have many memories there, too, but because of lack of space will comment on only one recollection that involved chewing tar that had just been laid down by street resurfacing crews. It was almost as good as the store-bought chicle (Blackjack or some such brand), and my friends and I all agreed on the supposition that it was great for whitening teeth. I can't really recommend it at this stage in my life, though, nor can I put in a good word for whooping cough as a weight loss tactic. You'd probably be better off going with Jenny Craig.

Prescott Courier, late 1990s

4

TAR CHEWERS UNITE IN DEFENSE OF YOUTHFUL HABIT

"I also chewed tar off the street despite the fact that Mom always scolded me and predicted I'd get some horrible disease–which I did–but I don't think scarlet fever had any connection to street tar!"
—Virginia Baker

A couple of columns ago I mentioned a childhood habit involving tar chewing. You know–the newly laid variety fresh out of the steaming cauldron manned by a City of Lubbock paving crew. Or, on extremely hot days, peeling off a glob of the stuff from pre-existing street work.

Well, wife Pat looked down her little nose at the practice. "It's *petroleum,* for cryin' out loud!" is the way she put it, implying that I probably should have died from it, or at least become deathly ill, neither of which occurred. In fact, to this day I sincerely believe that it had a salutary effect by helping to whiten my teeth. (No, that's carrying it a bit far. What it really did, as I recall, was to make them less yellow.)

Three readers who, like me, are former tar-chewing addicts responded to the column. I assume they've all kicked the habit by now. I know I have. But they did provide some riveting commentary regarding the practice.

There was that letter to the editor, for example, from a Prescott lady, Virginia Pannkoke, who said she was surprised to learn that anyone else had chewed hot tar. She said she is more than 70 years old and is a native of Phoenix, where "any tar used to patch the cracks in the pavement would be hot from May through October." As a schoolchild, "we would reach down and pinch off some tar to chew. We were very careful not to step in it in the hottest part of the summer because it would stick to our feet and burn. The tar's temperature was perhaps 140. Those were the 'good old days.' Perhaps the temperature of the tar killed any germs."

There also was an e-mail from Prescott's Jabe Wills, who was born and raised in Hereford in the Texas Panhandle, near Amarillo. He said that nostalgia from my West Texas childhood "mirrors much of mine" and that "I was specifically struck with your account about chewing the tar from the streets. Having heard me relate the same memory from digging out the tar between the (brick) streets of Hereford, my wife still looks at me with great skepticism each time the topic comes around." (I can believe that!)

Speaking of Hereford, during my growing-up years my parents always referred to it as "the town without a toothache" because of its reputation for super drinking water. Now, I've known only one person who hailed from Hereford–a girl I met in college–and her dad was a dentist there, which I've always thought was ironic. Be that as it may, though, there's no doubt but that its water was of much better quality than Lubbock's, which was hard and, after years of imbibing, tended to stain teeth (the lower half, mainly) brown. How hard was Lubbock's water? Well, when a person took a drink and it hit the bottom of his stomach, it would go "klunk!" (I made that

5

up, but you must believe me when I say that the town's water was indeed lousy because of what it would do to people who made the mistake of overdosing on it.)

And then there was a letter from a friend from way back who is a former Prescott resident now living in Scottsdale, Virginia Baker, who confessed that "I also chewed tar off the street despite the fact that Mom always scolded me and predicted I'd get some horrible disease–which I did–but I don't think scarlet fever had any connection to street tar!"

Anyway, I'd like to respond to her by saying that yes, Virginia, there *IS* a Sanity Clause when it comes to tar chewing. It exists as certainly as the Internet and DVDs. Alas! How dreary would be the world if there were no tar chewing! It would be as dreary as if there were no Virginias. Or Carolinas. Not believe in tar chewing?! You might as well not believe in fairies. Did you ever see fairies dancing on the lawn? Of course not, but that's no proof that they aren't there. And it's the same way with tar chewers, who you may never see, but in this world there is nothing else real and abiding! (With apologies to the New York Sun's Francis Pharcellus Church.)

Prescott Courier, undated, late 1990s

DAD—AND TOOTS—WOULD FIND THIS A HAPPY ENDING

Toots and Jerry, in his Tom
Sawyer outfit.

Surprisingly, about a month later Toots showed up at our front door. She had lost some pounds and her hair was all matted, but she seemed to be happy to be back home after what had to be an incredibly incredible journey spanning those 73 miles.

It happened more than 70 years ago, but I still remember waiting anxiously for my dad to come home from his job at the cotton compress so I could tell him what occurred right there in our front yard on Avenue J—just a few blocks from downtown Lubbock. I told him that Toots, our family pet, and another dog had somehow gotten "stuck together" and that I didn't know what to make of it. (Hey, what you must take into account is that I was only 5 or so years old at the time and not at all worldly.)

Anyway, Dad told me not to worry about it and went on about his business. Sometime later, though, Toots produced a litter of pups from the liaison, which she was prone to do periodically, and that "littering" habit came to be a concern for my mom, in particular, because it wasn't easy to find homes for the little critters as they kept coming onto the scene. The logical solution, of course, would've been to have Toots "fixed", but my parents were always strapped for money and chose not to spring for the expense of visiting a vet to accomplish the goal.

So what to do? Well, Dad had a younger brother who was serving as a Methodist preacher in tiny Bledsoe, 73 miles west of Lubbock, a couple of miles east of the New Mexico line, and when a parishioner heard of our family's dilemma offered to assume ownership of Toots. After all, her new home would be in a fenced yard, and prospects were that she would do well as a transplant. So Dad drove her over in our '37 Chevy, and the matter was resolved in compassionate fashion. Or so my parents thought.

Surprisingly, about a month later Toots showed up at our front door. She had lost some pounds and her hair was all matted, but she seemed happy to be back home following what

7

had to be an incredibly incredible journey spanning those 73 miles. What kind of radar can an animal possess to pull off such a stunt of loving loyalty? Needless to say, Toots remained part of our family until she passed away of old age years later.

Prescott Courier, October 2010

BACK TO LUBBOCK FOR OUR 45TH REUNION WAS A GOOD JAUNT

It somehow never dawned on him that Dean had the height, weight and reach on him, so Ross invariably came out on the short end of the stick.

I moseyed back to Texas in June, the occasion being the 45th reunion of Lubbock High's Class of '51. The nostalgia was flowing pretty fierce, of course, and there were people there I hadn't seen for, well, 45 years.

As we look back on our high school days, many of us recall a certain circle of friends . . . special people who enlivened our lives . . . and two-thirds of my good buddies of the era–Carl Ince and Ross Shelton of Texas and California, respectively, managed to make the scene. Only Earl Dietering, now a Tennessean, couldn't make it.

But three out of four isn't too shabby, so we had ourselves a quorum, anyway, for some yesteryear yammerings.

I must admit early on that I was sort of the fifth wheel of the foursome. Carl, you see, was a whiz-bang basketballer who played a big part in helping LHS to a state championship during our senior year. Ross, on the other hand, was a solid-as-a-rock guard on the football team, which was making it into the playoffs with regularity. And Earl was manager of the basketball team and could be counted on to supply the players with fresh towels when it came time to shower.

So each of them was doing something for the glory of the school, if you know what I mean. I just stood around a lot. Why, I was so puny that I couldn't even climb the rope in P.E.! I was simply an embarrassment all the way around. Still, though, I got invited to ride on the bus down to Austin with the basketballers when they nailed down that state title, probably out of compassion for my circumstances.

Ross was a funny guy armed with a wry sense of humor. Among other things, he and his dad were ham radio operators, and he had a habit of reciting the ham alphabet in a singsong manner that went: "Able Baker Charlie Dog Easy Fox George." Sort of catchy in a strange way.

I also remember the time when he, Earl and I went to see "Flying Tigers," starring John Wayne, at the Palace Theater. The Duke, of course, was the leader of his squadron, and every time he got ready to take off he'd glance over at the plane on his left and give that pilot the ol' thumbs-up sign, then look to his right and repeat the procedure. This happened *every time* he and his wingmen took off, which they did a whole lot of during the course of the flick.

Well, about the eighth time around, Ross mumbled, "Y'know, if he ain't careful he's gonna get that thumb shot off!"

Ross and I go back to elementary school, incidentally, where a daily ritual of his back then was to fight a classmate, Dean White, during the lunch hour. He just figured that it was his calling to mix it up with Dean as sort of a rite of passage, but it somehow never dawned on him that Dean had the height, weight and reach on him. So Ross invariably came out on the short end of the stick. But he'd rush back to school from lunch at home every day just for that purpose, and Dean would obligingly beat him up.

His dad started suspecting something when Ross would go barreling out of the house like that, though, and would ask him teasingly: "Son, have you got a girlfriend?" and Ross would reply, brightly, "Awwww, Dad!"

Ross, incidentally, is just as scrappy as ever, being a resident of–I kid you not–Rough and Ready, Calif.

Prescott Courier, November 1996

Road Pals Burned the Road; Mom Burned the Sheets

No sooner had Dad and Mom left the house than a bunch of Road Buddies converged on the place like moths to a flame, sensing a greater opportunity for an independent lifestyle than that afforded at their own parents' home.

Speaking from a personal standpoint, there were several other Texans in addition to Dubya who descended on Prescott last weekend. It was reunion time with a laid-back bunch of critters known loosely in our high school and college days as the Road Buddies of America, and they came all the way to Prescott for our 3rd annual reunion after huddling the previous two years back in the Lone Star State–in San Saba and Irving.

It was a time to reminisce . . .

There was Jack Weldon's car, for example–a plodding late '40s Buick with big teeth–you remember . . . coming at you the monster looked just like "Jaws," and it would go from zero to 60 in 4.5 minutes. But Jack was very proud of it for some reason.

Well, I had a much hotter car, a '49 Olds "88" whose engine roared with a certain panache. Its front end pointed down a bit and, when idling, it would just gurgle with a delight you can only imagine, straining at the bit to get on down the road.

Anyway, Jack and I got to discussing our respective vehicles one day, arguing about which one was better, and finally settled on asking another Road Buddy, Buzz Burkhalter, for a neutral opinion. Buzz looked at both cars, parked there side by side, and his answer came quickly and resolutely as he motioned to Jack's car: "You couldn't *give* me that one-lunged, anemic thing!" he responded, sincerely.

Jim Cromer, left, who loved eating and wasn't particularly particular when it came to the type of food put before him, shares a laugh with the author during an early-'50s outing in Ruidoso, N.M.

Then there was Paul Stuart, who arrived at Texas Tech from Paris (Texas, that is) on a football scholarship and was a handsome 6-4 who was catnip to the coeds. Paul was sort of an Adonis, being quite a bit better looking than the rest of us. I always hoped that some of that allure might rub off on me, by osmosis, but somehow it never came about.

But back to Jack, whose church-going habits were interesting back then. We all attended Asbury Methodist there in Lubbock, which was just a couple of blocks from Jack's home. The problem, though, was that Jack enjoyed sleeping in on Sunday morning a lot more than he did going to church. So when Paul and I would go over to try and roust him out, his tactic was to open one eye, roll over and say, "Sorry, but Mother doesn't like for me to go to church." If she happened to be within earshot, Mrs. Weldon–a good Christian woman–could only roll her eyes and cringe.

There was that summer, too, when my parents went down to Corpus Christi for six weeks and left me alone to look after things at our place there on Avenue R. (My dad, who worked as a weigher in a cotton compress in Lubbock, went to Corpus during the summer because the season down there was a couple of months ahead of Lubbock's and he could pick up some extra bucks that way.)

Well, no sooner had Dad and Mom left the house than a bunch of Road Buddies converged on the place like moths to a flame, sensing a greater opportunity for an independent lifestyle than that afforded at their parents' home.

Paul and his brother, Ben, were hanging out, as were James Sides, Bill Gaither and James Cromer. And in those six weeks that my parents were gone, none of us thought to bother to ever wash any dishes. Yeah, I remember one time when Ben was having a cup of coffee, and when he picked up the cup the saucer came with it because,,, well . . . it was pretty sticky on the bottom from previous use.

Actually, Bill was the only one of us who had any semblance of decency when it came to cleanliness, and we nicknamed him "Mama" for his efforts. He was our only cook, too, and did a commendable job in that regard, if only by default.

Bill provided innovation in his cooking, too. In fact, several of us were sitting around one day discussing eating habits and the like, and reached a consensus that Cromer–who wasn't around at the time–would eat *anything*. So, to test the theory, Bill whipped up a nice cornmeal pie (it had a cup of salt among its ingredients, and looked for all the world like a lemon pie to the unknowing), topped if off with some puffy meringue, and left it on the dining room table for Cromer to sample upon his return. And you know, he ended up wolfing most of it down and didn't complain even one little bit about the odd filling.

The thing I remember most vividly when my parents returned, though, was Mother going around to all the beds and ripping off the sheets, then burning them.

Personally, I think all those sheets were salvageable, but what do *I* know?

Prescott Courier, undated, late 1990s

CHANGE IS INEVITABLE, BUT MEMORIES WILL ALWAYS REMAIN

Nowadays I visit dentists on a quarterly basis, alternating between Dr. Wulff and Dr. Maupin, and seldom does either one of them have to chase me around the office to get me in The Chair.

The splendiferous structure that is Lubbock High School is on the National Register of Historic Places.

Jerry at age 5

Getting there–the "there" in this instance being a trip to Lubbock to attend my 55th high school class reunion–was part of the fun, as the saying goes. While sitting in a packed Southwest plane awaiting takeoff at Sky Harbor, for example, there was a cute comment from the stewardess who was giving the obligatory spiel on safety. (I still prefer the term "stewardess" because it is much more tantalizing; after all, "flight attendant" can also encompass hairy-legged guys who, though competent, are much less appealing visually.)

Anyway, what she did was to point out that the seat cushions can double as flotation devices and cautioned us to keep that in mind because we were about to be flying over a bunch of hot tubs and swimming pools. Then, when the plane landed in Albuquerque for a stopover, she cooed: "We know how lucky you are to have had us as your flight crew." (Here's to Southwest, for its ever-lovin' laid-backness!)

Seeing classmates from so many years ago was a hoot, of course, and the anecdotes focusing on "the way we were" came along hot and heavy. Mortality entered the picture, too, with recognition of the passing of more than one-fourth of our class of 408 graduates.

Lubbock itself, of course, has experienced a world of change over the years. And downtown, to tell the truth, has gotten long in the tooth stemming from the customary flight to the suburbs. For example, there is that one-time grande dame, the 11-story Lubbock Hotel, whose windows—many of them broken—stare blankly at Broadway, and plywood adorns the larger windows and entrances on the ground level.

Another example of downtown blight is the boarded-up Green Building on Avenue J, which formerly was the Myrick Building. As a pre-schooler I lived just three or four blocks from it. And it was there that my parents took me on my first visit to the dentist, which never reached fruition. You see, I ran for safe harbor under a couch in the waiting room—acting much more like a 3-year-old than a proper 5-year-old—and after a while my parents just gave up and took me home. (Nowadays I visit dentists on a quarterly basis, alternating between Dr. Wulff and Dr. Maupin, and seldom does either one of them have to chase me around the office to get me in The Chair.)

While driving around downtown, I made it a point to seek out Avenue H, in that the family home on that street—about a mile or so from downtown in a largely commercial and light industrial area—was my birthplace. Well, as fate would have it, Avenue H has been re-christened as Buddy Holly Avenue, and the street just to the east of it is now Crickets Avenue. (Geddit? Buddy Holly and the Crickets, a moniker that subsequently would inspire those lovable Liverpudlians to call themselves the Beatles.) Naturally, the family home, which was across the street from a machine shop and a Mobil filling station, is long gone, but the memories still linger.

One thing that hasn't changed, though, is that beautiful old building housing Lubbock High School. It has expanded, yes, while blanketing the campus with structures and spilling over onto an adjacent street that was closed off to permit construction of two gymnasiums. But all of the new construction remains true to the Italian Romanesque style of the complex that was completed in 1931 and is now on the National Register of Historic Places.

Lubbock High had its inception at another location in 1922, and the commemorative marker listing the seven school board members at the time was subsequently moved to the school's new location. Among those names etched into the concrete marker is Mrs. H.W. Sims, my grandmother, and the only female member of the board at the time. She and my granddad, Henry Walton Sims, lived out their days in their home at the corner of Avenue Q and 9th Street, directly across Q from the Holiday Inn that was headquarters for the recent LHS reunion. Not surprisingly, their home no longer exists, with a building housing an insurance firm now occupying the site.

Change is undeniably inevitable, but is incapable of burying memories. And they came back in a rush this month with that nostalgia-tinged visit back to the old hometown.

Prescott Courier, October 2006

FAMILY TRADITION CALLS FOR ZANY, WACKY BEHAVIOR

Jack Weldon

Those present confirmed that they'd never heard such moaning, groaning and grunting, before or since, as there was coming out of that bathroom.

Yeah, it WAS sort of a long way to drive for a birthday party. Nine hundred miles or so round trip, to be exact, as wife Pat and I took the southern route to Hobbs, N.M., last week and sandwiched in our first visit to Bisbee as an added attraction.

In case you're not familiar with Hobbs, it's in the southeastern part of the state and, when you drive east from there you almost immediately enter Texas and yet another time zone.

But that's where Jack Weldon's four daughters were putting on a surprise "70th birthday party" for their dad, who was turning 69. (I can't explain the discrepancy except to note that the Weldons are an unorthodox family and that all members of same are to be taken lightly.)

Unorthodoxy does indeed run rampant in the family. Jack's dad, for example, ran a used car lot in Lubbock many years ago, and was an accomplished trader who wouldn't pass up a deal just because a customer was lacking in cash. So it is that he once swapped a well-used car for five gallons of peanut butter. (Jack remembers it well, recalling that his family eventually got pretty sick of peanut butter preparations in all their various forms.)

On another occasion, Papa Tom traded one of those 6-foot-tall Coke machines to his barber for a year's worth of haircuts.

Anyway, the nostalgic anecdotes were falling like rain during Saturday's bash at a Baptist church there in Hobbs and also during a gathering of friends the night before at the home of one of Jack's sisters. Space will allow the telling of only two of the yarns, though.

First, there was the time when Jack, still in his feisty teens, was preparing to throw a party at his home in Lubbock when his parents were away and he expected them to stay that way. So it naturally came as a shock when his mother unexpectedly appeared at the front door after Jack had gone to the trouble of icing down a lot of beer in the bathtub. And compounding his dilemma was the fact that his mom was a teetotaltarian (not a word, but rather a lifestyle), so Jack came up

15

with some quick thinking by dispatching his kid brother, Donald (six years his junior) into the bathroom with whispered instructions to make a lot of appropriate noises until Jack could send their mom on her way. Those present confirmed that they'd never heard such moaning, groaning and grunting, before or since, as there was coming out of that bathroom that night.

The other happening occurred back in the '50s, and Gene Chance–a teammate of Jack's on the Midwestern University football team in Wichita Falls, Texas–described the episode in graphic detail.

Jack was captain of the team when it visited Tempe to take on what was then Arizona State College. In addition to quarterbacking the team, he also was the kickoff return guy and–prior to the opening kickoff–told his teammates that he intended to run it back for a touchdown. This, he reasoned, would get the drop on the Sun Devils early on and might even pave the way to a Midwestern victory.

Sad to say, though, it didn't work out as planned. As Chance told it, Jack cradled the ball and was high-tailing it at top speed when a player named John Jenkins–whose biceps, Chance noted, were the diameter of telephone poles–simply stuck out an arm and "clothes-lined" Jack, sending him reeling to the turf like some sort of rag doll. Despite that disastrous debut, though, Chance said that Jack went on to quarterback the team the entire game, although he could remember only three of the raft of plays in his playbook.

I asked Chance about the outcome of the contest, and he confirmed that it was indeed a terrible time in Tempe. "We got whipped pretty bad," he said. "In fact, we just barely made it home from the game!"

Prescott Courier, October 2002

TAKING A TRAIPSE DOWN MEMORY LANE

Jankans was "a very nice man who was without a doubt the dominant football player for Arizona State in that era."
—Norb Wedepohl

I received some sustenance from the feedback trough last week following publication of Tuesday's column describing the adventuresome spirit of an old friend of mine, Jack Weldon, while he was quarterbacking, and kick-returning, for the Midwestern University team out of Wichita Falls, Texas.

I had described, in semi-sordid detail, Jack's return of the opening kickoff in a game in Tempe against then-Arizona State College that took place back in the '50s. His admirable goal was to run it back for a touchdown, but—as noted in the previous column—things went terribly wrong when a Sun Devil I identified as John Jenkins extended an arm (featuring biceps the diameter of telephone poles) and "clothes-lined" the nimble Jack. The maneuver zonked him out for the rest of the game, but he still managed to get through it, albeit shakily.

Norb Wedepohl, a longtime Prescott resident who was the clerk of Superior Court for Yavapai County until his retirement this past December, provided the aforementioned feedback. He shed some light on the gridder who laid Jack low, including clarifying his name: make it John Jankans, not John Jenkins.

Norb, who enrolled at Arizona State in 1953, remembers Jankans well, noting that he hailed from Pennsylvania and that he was a Sun Devil starter for four years running. He was a perennial All-Border Conference selection at defensive tackle and, Norb noted, was "a very nice man who was without a doubt the dominant football player for Arizona State in that era."

Moving right along to the "small world" category, I asked Norb if he remembers Tom Shively, a quarterback with Arizona State at the same time that Jack got his comeuppance. Yes, he replied, and recalled sitting in on at least one class with him.

Well, Tom—formerly of Connecticut and now of Roseville, Calif.–is my son Kerry's father-in-law. And he too remembers the outstanding playing talent that Jankans—whose nickname, he said, was "City"–displayed there at ASC.

Dan Devine was head coach during his playing years, he added, and Frank Kush was line coach. After leaving Arizona State, Devine went on to coach at the University of Missouri, for the Green Bay Packers and at Notre Dame University, whereas Kush subsequently took up the reins as head coach at Arizona State.

By: Jerry W. "Slats" Jackson

Tom also came up with the score in the previously mentioned game—one in which a teammate of Jack's, Gene Chance, recalls that "we got whipped pretty bad." The year was 1955, and the score was: Arizona State 28, Midwestern 7.

Prescott Courier, October 2002

ORGANIZER AGONIZED OVER FINDING SENIOR TRIP SITE

Shucks, they could have gone to Sodom and/or Gomorrah if that was their choice...

Some serendipity surfaced one night last week when the phone rang. The voice on the other end of the line inquired: "Is this the person to whom I am speaking?" Pat confessed to that being the case, and then said: "This sounds like Jack Weldon."

Then the guy responded, sort of pseudo-testily, that "I know who *I* am. I've got my I.D. right here. But who are *you?*"

That's Jack for you. Unpredictable but definitely delightful. He's an old high school buddy whose mind tends to work in mysterious ways.

For example, when I got on the line he said that he was calling to pass along some good news, and I thought at first that he had decided to include me in his will or something. But that wasn't even close. Instead, he said he had read a recent article that said every seven and a half seconds, on average, somebody in the United States reaches the age of 50. And that prompted Jack to think–in a masterpiece of convoluted logic–that the two of us, both in our mid-60s–might somehow revert to that age because of the prevalence of the phenomenon. Being 50 again, he reasoned, would make us both feel better about ourselves.

Then the topic veered to high school class reunions. (We both made the 45th anniversary of the Class of '51 and–if the creeks don't rise–will no doubt be in Lubbock for my 50th in 2001.)

Anyway, Jack told me a story I'd never heard before about his senior trip back at Lubbock High. (I graduated in the spring of '51, but Jack didn't glom onto his diploma until January of '52.)

Now January, in West Texas, is not always pleasant from the standpoint of weather. So those '52 grads opted to wait until the following summer to take their trip, and Jack somehow got the assignment to pick the destination. The only stipulation was that it be no more than a specified number of miles from Lubbock. The school administration would not consider granting an overnighter, thinking–rightly or wrongly–that going along with such a request would inevitably lead to fully half the class returning from the excursion as expectant mothers.

That discriminatory practice is something that bugged me all the way through school, because all those kids in the farming communities around Lubbock would start saving up for their senior trip while they were still in their baby crib, and when the time came they would hop a plane for someplace like Tahiti or Rio de Janeiro. Shucks, they could have gone to Sodom and/ or Gomorrah if that was their choice, and you know why? Well, it's because each graduating class was made up of only four or five kids on average, with each having at least one parent on the school board. And those parents knew full well that their little darlings would never engage in anything untoward while on the trip.

All of us kids at LHS were very sophisticated, of course, and looked down our noses at the farm kids, calling them all sorts of politically incorrect names like "hicks" and "plow boys." But deep down, we harbored an intense jealousy relating to the Senior Trip Freedom Syndrome, which they flaunted mercilessly.

Well, Jack, as Locator-in-Chief, proceeded to take a drawing compass, placed the pointy thing on Lubbock, and drew a circle in the prescribed radius. And the spot he picked, he said, was a place on the farthest reaches of the circle–some burg called Sligo. (I can't confirm this, but Jack may very well have been the inspiration for that song about happiness being "Lubbock in the rearview mirror.")

Space will not permit me to go into the detail I'd like regarding Jack's choice, so stay tuned for next week's update on how it all turned out. I can guarantee that it'll tug at your heartstrings.

Prescott Courier, March 1999

TEXAS PLACE NAMES POSE PLENTIFUL PUNSTER POTENTIAL

If any of you wants to draw up an intentional disaster plan for a school trip, Jack would be a good person to contact.

Last week I wrote about my old high school buddy, Jack Weldon, and how Lubbock High's officialdom commissioned him to choose the spot for the class trip of the mid-term graduates of January 1952.

(They took the trip in the summer of '52 when the weather was more agreeable.)

And now, like Paul Harvey, I bring you The *Rest* of the Story.

You may recall how school officials limited Jack's choice of site to a specific maximum number of miles from Lubbock, fearing a passel of potential pregnancies should the class receive overnight dispensation. So Jack simply took a drawing compass and made a circle around Lubbock, then started looking for a spot that would be the farthest away to qualify under the edict. And what he came up with was Sligo, Texas.

In retrospect, Jack could probably have done better, but–to his credit–he did investigate by phone and found out that Sligo had a roller skating rink and a public swimming pool. When he and his classmates arrived, though, they discovered that the rink had been closed for years. (The wooden floor's boards were all curled up and gnarly–the place was a mess.) The swimming pool had only two feet of water in it, and in addition to being shallow had a definite greenish tint.

That was bad enough, but to top it all off Jack and the girl he was madly in love with at the time were on the outs and didn't even sit together on the bus, coming or going. They just exchanged occasional icy stares.

So if any one of you out there wants to draw up an intentional disaster plan for a school trip, Jack would be a good person to contact.

Sligo doesn't even exist in the modern era. Maybe Jack consulted a map printed before the place dried up and blew away in one of those fabled West Texas windstorms. (My map's liberal listing of place names jumps from Slidell to Slocum.)

Sligo aside, Texas has a lot of exotic place names such as Paris, Italy, Palestine, Egypt, Orient, Moscow, Tokio, Nazareth and Eden, the latter being a real garden spot. But most of them fell outside Jack's mandated compass radius. Heck, there's even a Heckville right there in Lubbock County, but nobody would be caught dead there.

Just for the fun of it I researched the map index, going cross-eyed over the tiny type that included more than 2,300 names ranging from Abbott to Zion Hill, and came up with some startling findings.

Examples: Halfway, Midfield and two Midways. Cee Vee. (Not to be confused with our own Chino Valley.) Lazbuddie. Mobeetie. Wink, which appropriately enough is in Winkler County, just to the east of which is Notrees in barren Ector County. We have Needmore and Progress, both in Bailey County, where Muleshoe is the county seat. And their needing more progress in Bailey brought to mind Dacosta and Dinero, with da costa dinero being quite reasonable nowadays, thanks to low interest rates. Those struggling to get by could always move to Cheapside, though. Or maybe Dime Box.

By all rights, Flat and Flatonia should be on the West Texas plains, but aren't. There's a Concrete, inhabited no doubt by solid citizens. And a Converse, where the talk of the town is the town of the talk. There's Topsey, which I hear is growing. Sunrise and Sunset. (If you were a rich man, you might consider moving to one of those towns.) Telegraph and Telephone. (No Cellular yet, but watch this space.) Quicksand, where you'd best not stand in one spot too long.

For the young at heart, I give you Joy, Happy, Jollyville and Utopia. For lispers, there's Goldthwaite. And then there's Okra. Quitaque, Pluck. Fairy. Gun Barrel City. Cut and Shoot. Tuxedo, Noodle. Magnet (to which residents are mysteriously drawn). And Fluvanna, which is definitely curable with the right antibiotics.

My favorite? It has to be a wee burg on the shore of Caddo Lake, which slops over into Louisiana. My guess is that they weren't all that sure if the town was in Texas or Louisiana, so they named it: Uncertain.

Prescott Courier, March 1999

BEHIND ALL THAT DARKNESS, COULD A SUNRISE BE LURKING?

The compassion didn't stop with the war's end, either, as Dad and Mom would box up and send "CARE packages" to some of the former POWs after they had returned home.

My parents, Walker and Cecil Jackson,
were compassionate souls.

I have this feeling deep down, that I simply can't shake. (And, for that matter, don't really want to.) The feeling is that the forces of Good, in the final analysis, will somehow buck the odds and triumph over Evil.

Granted, the prospects are not encouraging, for at this very moment there no doubt are atrocities of one sort or another being committed somewhere in the world in the name of patriotism. Or purification. Or religion. And there's the constant reminder that we live in a nuclear age, with its unprecedented potential for obliterating our species and all other species in the line of fire.

Still, though, there remain a lot of very good people Out There among the not-so-good and the truly bad. My dad was one of those good ones, though, and I'd like to share with you some reminiscences in that regard.

Dad's life work was as a weigher in a cotton compress in Lubbock, Texas. He would weigh the bales after they arrived from the gin and see that they were sampled and then properly stored prior to compressing and shipping by rail at a later date.

The year, as I recall, was 1944, and a major portion of the workers he had under him were German and Italian prisoners of war who were bused to the compress each day from the air base where they were housed. The arrangement worked out nicely, too. It gave the POWs something meaningful to do with their time and also provided the government with some revenue from the compress owner for services rendered.

The prisoners were treated humanely, of course, but not coddled, which is precisely how it should be under the circumstances. But my dad, soft-hearted sort that he was, did what he could to help ease the plight of the men who, like our own servicemen taken prisoner, were lonely and wanted only to return to their homeland as soon as the shooting war was over.

So, for example, if Dad noticed that the bread they were rationed for lunch was a bit moldy, he would try to make it a point to bring along a fresh loaf or two the next day to pass along to them for sharing. "Officially," that sort of thing was frowned upon, but the guards were kind enough to "look the other way" at convenient times so that Dad could do his thing unhindered.

Some might view his actions as "fraternization with the enemy," but I know otherwise. And I would only hope that there were some "Walker Jacksons" in Germany, or wherever our own GIs were held prisoner, who acted in similar fashion. There simply had to be some humanity present outside Dachau, Buchenwald and Treblinka.

The compassion didn't stop with the war's end, either, as Dad and Mom would box up and send "CARE packages" to some of the former POWs after they had returned home, knowing how conditions must have been in their own devastated land.

They were grateful for the kindnesses shown, and wrote letters of appreciation. Here is one of those letters, typewritten Sept. 28, 1946, from Milan. It is repeated verbatim in order to retain the warmth and sincerity conveyed:

"Dear Sir Jackson,

"I write you with delay but believe me I did not forget you, on the contrary, I often spoke, with the others my fellows, about you and remembered you with pleasure. We have not forgotten your kindness and your good words to us war-prisoners and with my fellows I thank you very much.

"I found my house undamaged and my parent in good health. At first it seemed to me no true to be again a free citizen but then, in short, I got accustomed.

"The journey, in spite of the great tiredness, was very good. I am well, I work and I hope at once to take a wife. To you and to your land I think very often, and I have to allow it, with home-sickness. Here in Milan people live discreetly well, but by you it is an other thing, you want nothing and you have all cheaply, while by us, if we wish live a little discreetly, it is no enough what we earn.

"I hope that you, your wife, and your sons are well and I wish you a good continuation. Many wishes again for coming up with your objects. I hope to be remembered yet from you and receive at once a letter from you. Many greetings from me and the others Cotton-prisoners fellows to you and your work fellows.

"I shake your hand warmly.

"Your faithfully."

It was signed: *Angelo Calori*

Prescott Courier, August 1997

MEMORIES TURN TO DEAR OLD DAD

It's been 30 years since Dad passed away, but his integrity, loving-kindness and sense of humanity live on with those he left behind.

With Father's Day just around the corner, my thoughts turn to the sweetest guy I've ever known—my own dad, Walker Franklin Jackson.

Dad was born in March 1899 in Muncie, Ind., the second oldest in a family of eight siblings. (That 1899 birth date made it easy to remember his age. And ditto for my only grandson, who was born in January 2000, so for most of the year that little fellow is as old as the year itself.)

Dad wasn't an Indianan for long, though, as his parents moved from that state to eastern New Mexico when he was an infant. His father was in the drayage business, hauling goods from Portales to wherever by horse-drawn wagon, and the family home there was a half-dugout—an excavation waist-high or so featuring newspapers as wallpaper. Primitive, to be sure (he and his siblings would amuse themselves at mealtime, for example, by asking such things as "Where do I see 'Men's shoes, $1.95'?" and seeing who could zero in on the answer first), so it came as quite a relief when the family subsequently migrated to West Texas and moved into a real house at 19th Street and Avenue S in Lubbock.

Many years later—Sept. 1, 1939, to be exact—my family moved into our brand-new home two blocks away, at 20th and R. (House and lot cost $4,500, and my parents' monthly mortgage payment was $39.) So how do I, as a mere 6-year-old at the time, remember that precise move-in date? Easy. That was the day when the Nazis blitzed Poland and launched World War II in earnest, so the date stuck in my craw.

Now, all of this prefacing is meant to lay the anecdotal groundwork to provide an example of how Dad was such a kind, compassionate and generous man. (Read: Soft touch.) You see, Miller's grocery was across Avenue S from his parents' homestead, and the store was where my sister, brother and I (mainly "I" as the "baby" of the family who was pretty much spoiled rotten) got into the habit of abusing a charge account that my parents maintained there. We simply signed the receipt for all manner of candy, ice cream, cookies and the like (it's a diet that I've struggled to maintain throughout my life and have done quite well with it, thank you), and Dad would cope with our extravagances by paying off the bill at the end of every month. This wasn't easy, either, based on the monthly $165 that he was earning as a weigher at the cotton compress, but never once did he complain or suggest that we back off from our addiction.

Growing up in the Jackson household was an enjoyable experience. Things could get manic on occasion, though, thanks to my brother Gene, the resident clown, and the joy he derived from pestering my sister Shirley just to hear her scream. (Gene was eight years older than me and five years older than Shirley, and those of you who have older brothers know how they can be.)

Well, one night the badgering had been going on for some time when Dad, who just couldn't take it any longer, bolted out of his easy chair, put on his hat and blurted, "That's *it!* I've had it!

I'm just going to *leave!*" Gene noticed that Dad wasn't wearing a shirt, though, and came back with: "You mean you're going to leave . . . in your *undershirt?*" Then he topped it off with, "Hold up just a second, Dad, and I'll go with you!"

Needless to say, that wasn't quite what Dad had in mind, so he just heaved a huge sign and plopped back down into his chair, defeated.

It's been 30 years since Dad passed away, but his integrity, loving-kindness and sense of humanity live on with those he left behind. He's right up there at the top of my personal "extra special" list.

Prescott Courier, June 2006

MATH PROBLEMS INCREASE USE OF ORANGE NEHI

It was plane geometry back at Lubbock High that was responsible for drumming me out of the National Honor Society.

When it comes to column writing, I must admit to being a Herronaholic. That's because whether the topic focuses on religion, mathematics or a senseless war, Al Herron provides carefully crafted insights that invariably coincide with what I'm thinking but which I can't state anywhere near as well.

A column of his a while back zeroed in on the practice of cramming scads of math into students, the vast majority of whom will not one day become scientists or engineers. Consequently, few of us grow up to be Einsteins, so most of the so-called knowledge in that regard goes for naught.

Prescott reader Paul M. Klein responded to Al's column in a letter to the editor this past Thursday when he noted that "fifty some-odd years ago my high school geometry teacher beat it into our heads that we will use geometry throughout our lifetime, so we had better learn it well. So far I have never used geometry in my daily life; basic math and business math yes, but never geometry."

I can certainly identify with that, as it was plane geometry back at Lubbock High that was responsible for drumming me out of the National Honor Society. (Hmpf.) You see, getting a "C" in any subject was the NHS kiss of death and I came up guilty as charged. I really can't blame Miss McCarty for the lapse, though, as she was a dear person who did her best to further my comprehension, but to no avail. In fact, the only thing I remember from the entire cussed course was "SAS equals SAS" and its soul mate, "ASA equals ASA." Translated, it equates to: "side angle side equals side angle side" and "angle side angle equals angle side angle." It had something to do with triangles and maybe even trapezoids, but I've never been able to use the knowledge to any sort of advantage.

I never warmed up to algebra, either, which was another required subject at LHS. But the most nightmarish tussles in math for me predated my high school experience and concerned those stated problems in the back of my sixth grade textbook. You know the ones I'm referring to: "If a train leaves New York City at 4 p.m. traveling 60 miles per hour and another leaves Chicago at the same time going 65 mph, will they collide in western Pennsylvania or eastern Ohio?"

Questions like that drove me to drink, which was orange Nehi at the time.

Prescott Courier, February 2007

DUST BOWL, YOU SAY? 'SAND BOWL' TELLS IT BETTER

I'd rather call it a SANDstorm, which denotes "true grit" as opposed to "dust," which we tend to think of only as that pesky stuff that settles on the shelves in our homes. (That's why they call it sandpaper; you never hear about dustpaper.)

Wild weather can crop up anywhere, of course, but it sure seemed to come around with more regularity back on the plains of West Texas during my long-ago years there. As the saying goes, it's where "the wind blows, the oil flows and the cotton grows," which pretty well capsulizes it.

Ah, yes, the wind . . . There was a reminder this past Friday of the damage it can cause when a photo accompanying a weather story showed part of a 23-vehicle pile-up five miles north of Post (which is 40 miles southeast of Lubbock) that claimed two lives. The culprit? A dust storm. At least that's what the caption said. But I'd rather call it a *sand*storm, denoting "true grit" as opposed to "dust," which we tend to think of only as that pesky stuff that settles on the shelves in our homes. (That's why they call it sandpaper; you never hear about dustpaper.)

I point out this distinction because of an incident that occurred back in the early 1950s when I was working part-time figuring payroll for a construction company in Lubbock while attending Texas Tech. The bookkeeper for the firm, a friend of mine named Billy Phillips, had purchased a new Ford sedan at a dealership in Post–a beautiful pale green car that he drove back to Lubbock during one of those monster sandstorms. By the time he got home, the car had turned from green to pretty much silver, though. Sand, not dust, will do that.

There's another weather-related story that concerned BMFP Construction, the firm that Billy and I were working for. Among the structures it built while I was employed there were the Coliseum on the Tech campus and the Great Plains Life building in downtown Lubbock. The Coliseum served the community–and Tech's basketball program–well until the new Spirit West Arena opened a few years ago, but Great Plains–an 8- or 9-story structure–suffered a major hit circa 1970 when a tornado came roaring through and twisted the building like a pretzel. (Somehow, retrofitting allowed for the continued use of the structure, although I still think that it looked sort of funny and out-of-sorts the last time I visited the old hometown.)

That tornado, incidentally, claimed more than 20 lives. It also blew away the home of my sister and her family in north Lubbock (fortunately, they had a storm cellar), and took out my brother-in-law's electric shop off 4th Street, leaving only the concrete foundation.

But back to the aforementioned town of Post, which is halfway between Lubbock and Snyder and which I traveled regularly in the early '60s while toiling at my first newspaper job with the Snyder Daily News. One night I was driving Highway 84 toward Lubbock in dense fog in the approximate area where last week's traffic pile-up occurred. It is a divided highway, with two lanes in each direction.

I was driving in the right-hand, or slow, lane when another car heading south glided past me, its driver obviously disoriented by the fog.

Whew . . . close call. Had I been in the passing lane I would be pushing up daisies now instead of boring you with these tales of bygone days.

Prescott Courier, February 2004

West Texas sandstorms come in colors, too

There was no keeping the sand out of houses, either, as it would somehow filter in to the point of even coating dishes in my mom's closed kitchen cupboard!

Granted, it's a gritty subject. But last week's little treatise on West Texas sandstorms prompted some welcome feedback.

The insidiousness of the storms is really something to behold, and prompted this recollection from reader Carol Mitchell: "I can remember as a child at my grandparents' little farm (near Lubbock), they had only one light bulb that hung from the ceiling," and "the sand was so bad you could hardly see the light."

I can believe that, and can recall vividly those "black dusters" of the dust bowl '30s when the sand would hang eerily in the air and it would become as dark as night so that I could just barely make out the outline of the houses across the street at my home in Lubbock. And there was no keeping the sand out of houses, either, as it would somehow filter in to the point of even coating dishes in my mom's closed kitchen cupboard! (See "insidiousness" above.)

Then there was this response from reader Vita Rinewalt: "Just wanted to say 'thanks' for starting my day with a smile! I spent 10 years in Lamesa, Texas, and will never forget my first experiences with a 'red' sandstorm. It's much nicer remembering what they were like than living with them!"

"Red" sandstorm? Well, yes, as evidenced by this update on the most recent monster blow from Bettie Hall, a fellow Class of '51 Lubbock High School classmate who remains a resident there. Her e-mail, on another topic altogether, ended with: "Had one heck of a nasty sandstorm this past week. Twenty-car pile-up on the Post highway with two deaths. Also a pile-up on the Tahoka highway with injuries. Combined there were 17 people taken to the hospital.

"Most of the sand at the beginning was dark red from New Mexico and it was zero visibility for nearly two hours. Finally it became Texas dirt and the sky lightened up but continued to blow until nearly dark."

Thank you, New Mexico, for the contribution. And there is yet another N.M. reminiscence from Prescott's Bill Parker, whose roots go back to Clovis, which is just a hop, skip and jump west of the Texas line.

Bill, taking note of last week's reference to the sandblasting that did in the paint job on a brand-new Ford sedan that a friend of mine drove in a sandstorm from Post to Lubbock, mentioned a common phenomenon back then that would be most noticeable after the worst of the spring windstorm season had mercifully gone thataway. There were a lot of cars being driven around with shiny all-silver front license plates, he recalls, along with those less-than-perfect paint jobs.

Oops. Space won't permit one other anecdotal rundown from another reader, so will pigeon-hole that one until next week. After that, taking into account that you no doubt will have had it with sandstorm stories by then, I'll swear–on a sack of black-eyed peas–to cool it on the subject, OK?

Prescott Courier, March 2004

THERE'S IRRITATION WITHOUT IRRIGATION

"Dad informed us that we were not going to eat another meal in Texas. We had breakfast near Roswell, N.M."
—Carl Trease

oving right along into the final installment of the trilogy on West Texas particulate peppering, join me as we venture into the eye of the sandstorm with a recollection from Prescott reader Carl Trease.

Carl tells a story that he has no doubt tried, without success, to forget. It's a homily, with grit (not to be confused with hominy with grits), that truly tugs at the ol' heartstrings. Here is his tale of woe:

"In June 1953, I was a 13-year-old lad, traveling with my family to visit my mother's folks in Phoenix. We dropped my father's mother off in Marshall, Texas, and turned west in the mid-morning. The route would take us through Dallas, Ft. Worth and across the West Texas plains.

"The third day out, we came upon a scene out of 'The Grapes of Wrath'. Being from the normally green landscape of Ohio, the brown, dusty unplanted fields were a shock. Dad enlightened us young ones in the back seat about the dust bowl of the '30s. This was a little bit of that tragedy.

"Soon we came upon a road grader that was scraping the wind-blown sand dunes off the highway–blown there the day previous, as there was precious little cooling breeze this day. We were doing all of 15 mph! There was no point in passing, of course, as it would be just a few yards until we would be stopped by the next two- to three-foot-high drift of sand. So, for miles, we followed this grader, 15 mph in an area where a normal person would have wanted to drive at 100 mph and get out of there.

"Did I mention that it had to be 120 F., and we were in an Ohio car without air conditioning?

"Finally, up ahead, was a general store next to the highway. My father's comment as we pulled in was that we needed a break, the car needed gas . . . and that grader needed to get down the road.

"As we walked back outside onto the front porch of the store, drinking a bottle of pop, Dad struck up a conversation with three gents wearing denim bib overalls and straw hats, leaning in straight-backed chairs against the shaded store front.

"Dad asked what they did for a living. One replied that they raised cotton. Now, a quick glance told everyone that the only thing green was the bottom of Dad's 1952 Ford–that same pale green that you used to describe your friend's Ford. Dad said that he did not see any cotton. Indeed, nothing was growing out of the ground, as far as the eagle eye of a 13-year-old could see, in any direction. 'Oh, we haven't planted any,' one responded. 'We're waiting for rain.' 'When did it rain last?' asked my dad. 'Three years ago,' said one. They just sat there, watching their fields blow from one side of the road to the other.

"We spent that night out in West Texas somewhere. Dad woke us kids up at O'Dark Thirty. He and Mom were dressed. We were told to get ready quickly, and not to expect breakfast for a while. Dad informed us that were not going to eat another meal in Texas. We had breakfast near Roswell, N.M."

Roswell, eh? At least you and your folks didn't end up getting spirited away by some aliens, Carl.

And that reference to cotton growers needs a bit of elaboration. You see, the West Texas plains are big in cotton farming, I note balefully, but only among those growers who have irrigation. Otherwise you're up the creek without a paddle. (Oops. The creek just dried up. But you've still got your paddle.)

Needless to say, it doesn't take dryland farmers too long to figure out that bringing in a crop every third or fourth year doesn't put many beans on the table.

And all that plowed-up irrigated land plays a vital role in making West Texas the Sandstorm Capital of the Universe, with the possible exception of Saturn.

Prescott Courier, March 2004

Yes indeed, Mr. Disney, this IS a small world

"I guess you're a pretty good old simpleton, really. It's just that you're a peasant...Anyway, good luck, you pigeon-toed, polka-dotted swine!"
—David Clark's touchy-feely yearbook testimonial

Yeah, that "It's a Small World" ditty is right on the mark. This came home anew to wife Pat and me last week when we vacationed in Colorado and visited a boyhood friend of mine–someone I hadn't seen in at least 45 years.

He's David Clark–a guy who lived a few blocks from me in Lubbock. We were in the same grade at Dupre Elementary, and would mosey over to each other's houses on occasion and cogitate on what was gong on in the world around us–or at least our little neck o' the woods.

As noted, I hadn't seen David since 1955 or so, when we both graduated from Texas Tech after going through grade school, junior high and high school together. He penned this poignant send-off in my '51 high school yearbook:

"I guess you're a pretty good old simpleton, really. It's just that you're a peasant. No kiddin' though, I have really enjoyed going around school with you and I hope we can continue our friendship through our lives. Anyway, good luck, you pigeon-toed, polka-dotted swine!"

(David always has had a way with words.)

Well, after a stint in the Army, David went on to get his Ph.D. and ended up professing (in journalism and English) and administering at the University of Wisconsin and Stanford University before settling in at Colorado State University in Fort Collins prior to retiring and moving with his wife, Alice, to Bellvue, a bit of a burg just a stone's throw from Fort Collins.

But back to that "small world" thing. While reminiscing about the old days back in Lubbock I mentioned to Pat that David played on the tennis teams at Lubbock High and Tech back then (he was the No. 1 singles player at Tech), and Pat noted that she was on the tennis team at Odessa High School a few years later. David responded that Odessa High had been a particularly formidable opponent because of the school's crackerjack coach, a man named Bob Clark.

"Did you know him?" he asked Pat. "Oh, yes," she replied. "He was my coach!"

A while later, while taking into account David's tenure at Colorado State, I mentioned that a Courier colleague of mine is a Colorado State alum who at one time worked for the *Fort Collins Coloradoan*. "Oh? Who was that?" he asked. "Tim Wiederaenders," I replied.

"Tim," he responded, "was one of my students!"

Like I said leading in, it's a small world after all.

Prescott Courier, September 2003

NOW, THAT'S A WHOLE LOT OF SINNING GOING ON

"I have seen a woman in Timnath of the daughters of the Philistines: now therefore get her for me to wife."
—Samson

Actually, I thought I was coming along pretty well in that Christian Believer class down at the church. That is, until I took a detour into disbelief a while back based on one of the daily readings.

It involved one of those mind-blowing references that an 18th-century poet-cleric and hymn writer, Augustus Toplady, came up with relating to sin. Seems that Toplady "carefully calculated how many sins a person was likely to commit in a lifetime of 80 years, and came up with a number in excess of two and one-half million."

As Jack Benny would say if only he were alive: " . . . WELL!"

Anyway, I whipped out the ol' pocket calculator and figured out that a person reaching the age of 80 will have lived 29,200 days (not counting leap years), and he or she would have committed 85.6 sins a day on average based on Toplady's calculation. (Frankly, I think that Toplady, who penned the words for "Rock of Ages," was a better lyricist than he was a mathematician.)

Now, I don't honestly think that many of us are measuring up to that sinning standard, even if you include dark thoughts in the mix. (I've had such thoughts on occasion, like when some guy cuts me off in traffic and then glares at me for having the audacity to share the road with him. But I don't gesture or anything like that when such an event occurs. After all, the guy may be packing a .38 or even a .45. Regardless, I nevertheless harbor a brief dark thought, which may well be a sin and would leave me with only 84.6 more for the day to measure up to Toplady's lofty sin peak.)

I would tend to equate Toplady's finding with that of an astronomer who announces that he has just discovered a star he has named Snicklefritz that is 863 light years away from Earth, and then defines a light year as one in which it would take an average human being 12,621 lifetimes of walking non-stop in order to get only halfway there. (I made up that analogy for dramatic effect, but you get the idea.)

Oh, well. That strange little detour shouldn't in any way detract from the Christian Believer class, which is made up of some interesting, inquisitive folks led by Jim Messerschmitt, who is a downright upright fellow in every respect. We bounce around all over the Bible in the class, of course, and there are some intriguing things that come out of it when we get together every Monday morn.

Just last week, for example, one of the daily Bible readings was Judges 14, focusing on Samson. Now, just about everyone knows the story of Samson and the cruel fate that Delilah, through the "shear" force of her personality, handed him. (Hair today, gone tomorrow.) As we all know, too, Samson was quite the physical specimen. In a drawing in my Bible showing him

35

working at the grinding mill following his downfall, in fact, he appears to be built just like Arnold Schwarzenegger, with muscles that would make Victor Mature look immature. Not only *that,* but Samson also *talked* like Arnold, as noted in my King James Version in the Judges 14:2 reference when he approached his father and mother and told them that "I have seen a woman in Timnath of the daughters of the Philistines; now therefore get her for me to wife."

Arnold couldn't have said it better himself.

Prescott Courier, undated, late 1990s

In Old West Anthology, Trails Lead Both Ways

"No, his only means of self-defense was his snappy little straw hat and his uncanny ability to speak only in sentences which, when spelled backwards, are exactly the same as when they were spelled forwards."
—Riders in the Sky's CD saga

The thing about palindromes (you know, they read the same forward and backward) is that *saying* them falls flat, since there's no way to absorb their legitimacy or validity. They simply *have* to be in black-and-white or they wallow in insignificancy. So here's a string of the things featuring a delightful bit of tomfoolery passed along to me by a Daily Courier paginating colleague, Tamra Larrabee.

The Western singing group known as Riders in the Sky put the soul-searching drama/song together, and it's a scream.

The lead-in is to the haunting strains of the "Paladin" theme song (remember the early-day TV series starring Richard Boone?), and goes like so:

There are campfire legends that the plainsmen spin
Of a man who was nothing like Pal-a-din . . .
Couldn't ride, couldn't shoot, but he won his fame,
'Cause everything he said, said backwards was the same . . .
Palindrome, Palindrome, what's in a name?
Palindrome, Palindrome, backwards the same.

Then the lilting music gives way to narrative in which a fellow speaking in a down-home monotone muses:

"Yes, Palindrome . . . No one knew where he came from and nobody cared. He rode into town one day from out of the west, armed not with six-guns, a long rifle, a whip, a knife, a chain saw or some other exotic weapon. No, his only means of self-defense was his snappy little straw hat and his uncanny ability to speak only in sentences which, when spelled backwards, are exactly the same as when they were spelled forwards."

Then came a scene "from an upcoming episode of 'Palindrome'," which led in with a female voice greeting the stranger in town with a "Howdy, stranger!"

Palindrome's reply: "Ma'am."

"Well, what's you name, pardner?" she asked.

""Madam, I'm Adam."

"Well," she continued, "How'd you get into town? I didn't see a horse."

"A . . . Toyota."

Then she yells to the bartender, "Hey, Doc, how about a drink for my new friend here?" and Doc acknowledged that "he sure could use it . . . look at his mouth hangin' wide open!"

Palindrome's suggestion: "In it ram a martini."

Doc: "Sorry, stranger, but there's no hard liquor here. But would you like some wine or some kind of beer?"

Palindrome: "Lager, sir, is regal."

Doc, compassionately: "You must be hungry . . . you're not trying to lose weight on one of them 'fasts,' are ya?"

Palindrome: "Doc, note, I dissent. A fast never prevents a fatness. I diet on cod."

Doc: "Sorry to tell ya, but we're out of cod. Look, you've got two choices–Italian or deli . . . what'll it be?"

Palindrome: "Go hang a salami; I'm a lasagna hog."

Doc: "Stranger, you've got a snappy answer for everything. But did you ever ask yourself a spiritual question?"

Palindrome: "Do geese see God?"

Finally, Doc had had about enough of it and said, "Stranger, I'm getting' tired of this!"

Palindrome shot back with: "Draw, O coward!"

The "mellow drama" ends with the captivated gal mentioned earlier exclaiming, "O, Palindrome, my hero! Would you join me in my room at noon for lunch?"

But Palindrome respectfully declines, manfully explaining that "sex at noon taxes."

What a guy!

Prescott Courier, March 2001

WHEN SELLING CARS, HONESTY ISN'T THE BEST POLICY

Jaguar ladies' noses are too long and unsightly, whereas hers is pert and just right. Anyway, you're not going to believe this, but she's a VEGA, for cryin' out loud, and is yours for $600.

Let's face it. I'm pretty lousy when it comes to selling cars. My own, that is. I base this on the fact that I come to know the vehicles intimately, am adept at detecting their flaws, and feel a responsibility to point out any quirks to prospective buyers so as to avoid selling them a bill of goods.

There was that gold-colored '74 Chevy Vega wagon I put up for sale back in the '80s, for example . . .

The ad read: "One owner. Hot; 0-50 in four minutes. One sick cylinder and addicted to cheap oil, but hey! Nobody's perfect. $600."

That ad didn't prompt many phone calls, so I tried this one: "Vega wagon. '74. Stick. Has some warts, which I'll explain in graphic detail, but she's lovable."

At the time those ads ran, I was toiling at the *Sacramento Bee* ("The Greatest Newspaper in the World Named After an Insect") and, for added exposure while seeking a buyer for the Vega, I whipped up a promotional blurb and posted it on the bulletin board at work. It read, in part:

"OK, you guys. I know you've been lusting after her body (by Fisher) for a long time now, drooling all over her out there in the parking lot. Although lovable, she's not perfect, of course, being addicted to 63-cent oil (Bel Air's muscatel) since they found some cancer cells in one of her cylinders. (I've been putting off having her operated on, in that the job's not covered by Metropolitan, Kaiser or Foundation Health Plan.) Also, her factory air gave up the ghost last year when her compressor died a horrible death . . . but I don't want to talk about it. She also smokes a little (Old Golds, naturally), but is trying to quit. Significantly, she has riveted side moldings (the glued-on factory types kept falling off) that are exciting to behold."

Then I lapsed into the car's most unique and exquisite feature–that jazzy hump down the middle of her hood–and expounded thusly:

"The only problem of a recurring sort I've ever had with her is that people are forevermore mistaking her for a Jaguar, which upsets and embarrasses her. Jaguar ladies' noses, see, are too long and unsightly, whereas hers is pert and just right. Anyway, you're not going to believe this, but she's a *Vega*, for cryin' out loud, and is yours for $600."

As I recall, I eventually sold the old girl for $450 or so. It was sort of painful, too, because she really had been faithful for a number of years and, along with her paint job, had a heart of gold beating within her shiny aluminum block.

By: Jerry W. "Slats" Jackson

Oops. With all of the above blathering about the Vega, I've run out of space to tell you about my ineptitude relating to the sale of my '79 Honda Accord and '69 Alfa Romeo Spyder convertible! But next week should be soon enough to deal with that trauma. So watch this space.

Prescott Courier, March 2003

Truth in advertising shouldn't run to car ads

So I placed this ad in the Sacramento Bee: *Spyder '69. Red ragtop $2,200. Carbon copy of Dustin Hoffman's in "The Graduate". Built like Raquel Welch, runs like Jim Fixx. (I know, he died!) Dream car for the true Alfisti who's into migraine headaches and self-flagellation.*

If I'm not mistaken, it was Elvis who recorded a big hit carrying the title "A Fool Such as I," and the title reminds me of my own situation when it comes to selling cars. And what better time than April Fools' Day (note: the column ran April 1, 2003, in Prescott's *Daily Courier)* to expand on my own perverse gullibility in that area?

Last week's odyssey focused on a '74 Chevy Vega wagon, and I promised to follow up today with some psychobabble about my experience in pursuing a buyer for a '69 Alfa Romeo Spyder convertible and a '79 Honda Accord. Soooo . . .

First, a bit of background on the Alfa, which I bought for my daughter in the late '80s while she was in college at the University of California in Santa Barbara. (I thought at the time that every coed should know the joy of bopping around in such a vehicle–she had expressed an Alfa interest on several occasions–and I certainly wasn't going to deprive her of the experience.)

The young fellow I bought the car from did his best to talk me out of it, cautioning me darkly that "unless your daughter has a boyfriend who's a good shade-tree mechanic, I wouldn't recommend that you buy this car for her." But I said (to myself, of course), what does he know? As it turned out, he knew quite a bit, and the car spent a lot of time in the shop, or at least huffing and puffing, for almost two years (and $2,200 or so in repair bills) before I threw up my hands and put it up for sale.

So I placed this ad in the *Sacramento Bee:*

Spyder '69. Red ragtop $2,200. Carbon copy of Dustin Hoffman's in 'The Graduate'. Built like Raquel Welch, runs like Jim Fixx. (I know, he died!) Dream car for the true Alfisti who's into migraine headaches and self-flagellation.

Didn't get any takers with that approach, so I discounted the sales price and went with this ad:

Alfa '69. Red ragtop. Runs off and on. Top's seen better days. Bit of rust on lower panels. But hey! Nobody's perfect! Needs understanding owner. $1,700.

I eventually sold the little critter to a guy for $1,300. He said he didn't care whether it was running or not, since all he wanted it for was the body. (Men are like that sometimes.) Anyway, he said he was planning to drop a new engine into it, replace the top, fix the rusted panels, repaint it and then surprise his wife with it.

Moving along, alphabetically, from the Alfa to the Honda, I bought that one from a young guy for $1,500 and immediately hit the road for Santa Barbara to transfer it to my daughter. I stopped at a restaurant for a bite to eat along the way, but when I got ready to resume the trip the car refused to go into reverse gear. So I pushed it away from the curb, put it in forward gear and completed the journey to my daughter's front door. And, after shelling out $850 for a transmission, she had a car that would go backward again on its own.

When it came time to sell that car, I ran this ad in the *Bee* under the heading "Imperfect Accord":

'79 4 dr. semi-automatic, air, AM/FM, but cassette's on the fritz, sunless roof, $899.95. Just spent $800 on her for repairs, only to learn she has a cracked crank, which sounds like a drug problem but isn't; she's running fine now, in fact, but one of these days will die unexpectedly, probably at 5 p.m. some Tuesday in the eastbound fast lane of Biz-80. Oh, she smokes, too, and isn't even trying to quit. If you think SHE"S bad, though, consider the '69 Alfa I squired around before her. That little redhead catted around town topless and ended up breaking my heart in two.

Again, no takers, but I *did* manage to sell it to a woman for $400 after running this follow-up ad:

Accord '79 4 dr., air, ps, am/fm cass., ugly but runs. Built like Danny DeVito. $600/ofr.

As I pointed out in last week's column, I'm not the sharpest knife in the drawer when it comes to selling cars.

Prescott Courier, April 2003

It was a snowy day on Prescott's Courthouse Plaza when wife Pat and daughter Shannon flanked son Kerry and his children–Emma, left, Fiona and Noah– for a photo op. (Noah's neck, incidentally, isn't broken, but instead is merely flexible.)

Pat poses beside the 1963 Chevy Impala that the author's parents purchased new. As of midsummer, 2011, she has 388,000-plus miles on her (the Chevy, that is, not Pat) and enjoys her addiction to 87 octane gas.

My late brother Gene, who served as an Army medic during World War II, received a commendation for his actions against the Japanese on Bougainville in the Solomon Islands.

Jerry and Pat share a happy moment during a Christmas party in Prescott's Pine Cone Inn in the late 1990s.

The author worked his way up to managing editor of the Prescott Courier in the 1960s before heading west to join the Sacramento Bee in 1968.

Jerry and Pat "tied the knot" Aug. 26, 1961, in the Bowman Chapel of Lubbock's First Methodist Church.

Jerry leans against his Chevy in front of his Lubbock home at 2003 Ave. R, where he resided from 1939 to 1955, when he was inducted into the Army.

TEXANS HAVE A GREAT DEAL TO BE IMMODEST ABOUT

This book review ran May 30, 1976, in the Sacramento Bee.

> *"Any man born in the United States is twice-blessed. And he is thrice-blessed if born in Texas."*
> —H. Ross Perot

THE TEXANS by James Conaway. Knopf; $8.95.

Texans, bless their hearts, have a well-earned reputation for thinking big and acting accordingly. James Conaway does absolutely nothing to dispel the notion, but he does lay bare a lot of warts in this absorbing narrative that reads like a novel.

Geographically, the power base of the state–along with its attendant wealth–is centered in Houston, Dallas and Austin. One might call it the Bermuda Grass Triangle for lack of a more coherent term. And, the book dissects the principals in the grandiose maneuverings that established and perpetuate that very power base.

. . . People such as John Connolly, who simply let his lease on the governorship lapse out of sheer boredom after serving three terms. He would go on to be appointed Treasury secretary by Richard Nixon in a move that, to a large degree, was window dressing. Here was a man who admitted knowing little about the workings of the Treasury Department and even less about economics. But he was, at that time, a Democrat–and his appointment created the illusion of bipartisan support for the administration.

Nevertheless, he proved to be an articulate spokesman who "provided an attractive and forceful personality unhampered by protocol or accountability, bypassing the men surrounding the President and earning their silent enmity. In the Nixon administration, Connolly stood out like a brass spittoon in a funeral parlor."

. . . People such as Sen. Lloyd Bentsen, who neither acts nor sounds like a Texan. Whereas Connolly, for instance, is quite capable of sprinkling his language with expletives for the sake of emphasis, Bentsen's rawest four-letter word is "crud." He leaves no doubt as to his goal, however. "I'm telling you as candidly as I know how," he told the author, "that I want to be President of the United States."

,,, People such as Lyndon Baines Johnson, who realized Bentsen's ambition.

There are thorns in the sides of politicians of all persuasions, and at one time LBJ's was in the unlikely form of the *Texas Observer*, a bi-weekly voice in the wilderness (circulation: 18,000) of the liberal political stance.

Johnson was a pained reader of the *Observer* and at one time summoned its editor, Ronnie Dugger, to a personal audience. In what the author described as a "sonorous snow job," Johnson tried to impress on him just how things are. To his dismay, though, Dugger proceeded to write up the meeting in his little paper. "You check that boy's family line," huffed LBJ, "and you'll find a dwarf in there somewhere."

. . . People such as H.L. Hunt, about whom J. Paul Getty would say: "The corporations in which I own shares are rich enterprises, but I am not wealthy. They hold the property, they control me. In terms of extraordinary independent wealth, there is only one man–H.L. Hunt."

Hunt was not without his eccentricities. Up until his death he showed up at his Dallas office on a daily basis, although confined to a wheelchair. It was common practice for him to bring his lunch along in a paper bag . . . and to park his old car blocks away to avoid those pesky parking fees.

. . . And people like H. Ross Perot, whose modest investment of $1,000 would blossom into assets estimated at $700 million in seven years on the crest of a computer boom.

He lost a lot of that when he personally tried to rescue Wall Street from one of its disasters. The appeal came from upstairs when Connolly petitioned Perot with: "The President would consider it a decent and patriotic act if you would intervene and help save the country from economic chaos."

It was a request that Perot could hardly refuse. After all, he once observed, "Any man born in the United States is twice-blessed. And he is thrice-blessed if born in Texas."

Shucks, you can't argue with logic like that.

—Jerry W. Jackson

INTEGRITY NEEDN'T BE OUTMODED

"Treasure the friend or family member who will be honest with you when all others tell you what they think you want to hear."

—Jim Messerschmitt

Jim Messerschmidt

In the dog-eat-dog business world we live in, proper ethics too often get lost in the pursuit of profit. Cutting corners and conniving are commonplace, and adhering to the Golden Rule often is viewed as a laughable mantra suggesting extreme naiveté. But it doesn't have to be that way. And I'd like to offer up Jim Messerschmitt's approach as proof.

Jim, now a Prescott resident, was fortunate to land a job in the 1960s with a fledgling company, Electronic Data Systems. The firm was headed by someone you've no doubt heard of, a fellow named Ross Perot. He and Jim share the same philosophy, which is to be tough and energetic in business dealings, but to never sacrifice one's ethics in those dealings.

Jim was immediately "hooked on the company and the people in it," he wrote in his autobiography, and "I guess they liked me. I was told that I was the 24th employee of EDS," he recalled, but upon his retirement 30 years later there were some 95,000 employees worldwide. "I never asked for a count of the number of EDS employees within my SBU (Strategic Business Unit), but I do know that my payroll was over a million dollars *a day.*"

Years after joining the company, he forwarded a note to Perot that stated: "I remember visiting with you shortly after I joined EDS and you said that your goal was to make all of us wealthy. You certainly did that from a monetary standpoint, but more importantly you gave us the opportunity to build wealth in character and job satisfaction."

When Perot launched EDS, "he determined that the company would function with very high moral and ethical standards," Jim wrote. "There would be no tolerance for an employee at any level who violated those standards. His reasoning was that if an employee would lie, cheat or steal in their private life, they would do the same thing with the corporation or a customer. There would be no room for slackers, poor performance, self-promoters or politicians (people who would try to get ahead at the expense of others)."

Consequently, "by setting the moral and ethical bar high, EDS attracted employees who already subscribed to those standards," Jim noted. And thus, "there was a warm sense of respect, trust and comradeship throughout the staff. We felt like, and worked like, a team."

Jim cites 16 "management truths" to live by. Space will allow only a few of them, but among them are:

- "A mirror provides the most effective performance evaluation you will ever receive."
- "Time is precious. Don't waste it trying to impress people with what you know. If they want to know, they will ask."
- "A great amount of productivity is lost trying to place blame. Define the problem, correct it, and move on."
- "An effective manager is a respected coach, not a dictator."
- "When you are wrong, apologize. When you are right, don't gloat or rub it in."
- "Treasure the friend or family member who will be honest with you when all others tell you what they think you want to hear."

To me, Jim's philosophy is mirrored in Kipling's classic poem titled "If", which closes with: "If you can fill the unforgiving minute with sixty seconds' worth of distance run; yours is the earth and everything that's in it, and–which is more–you'll be a man, my son!"

Jim, a former marathoner, has definitely put in his "sixth seconds' worth of distance run," and then some, and is continuing to write a primer of right living by his actions.

Prescott Courier, August 2010

'COVRT HOVSES' IN ATLANTA 'SVFFER' FROM TYPOS

You won't find it happening here in this county, because the "u's" engraved on the Yavapai County Court House are as round as a baby's bottom.

Actually, wife Pat and I shared some mild trepidation last week even before the plane lifted off from Sky Harbor for our trip to Atlanta to visit our daughter. (August in Atlanta? Well, it's not exactly April in Paris, but there's still a lot of incredibly lush beauty back there among the magnolias and Spanish moss in areas they haven't gotten around to paving over yet.)

Our concern stemmed from the very first sentence in the introductory greeting in the Frontier Airlines magazine tucked into the seat in front of us. It was from the president of the airline, who wrote: "Dear Frontier Customer: Approximately five years ago–July 5, 1999, to be exact–Frontier Airlines first took flight." That's all well and good, except that we were traveling in that self-same year (the column appeared in the *Daily Courier* on Aug. 17, 1999). So that set us off to wondering, right off the bat, about that particular airline's overall efficiency.

There was really no cause for worry, though. The only glitch during the whole trip resulted from the thunderstorms in the Atlanta area that initially backed up traffic, and then put all landings on hold. The captain got on the horn and advised everyone that he had two options. One involved circling Atlanta for maybe an hour and a half and that he might–or might not–have enough fuel to pull it off. The other was to set that big ol' 737 down in Macon on a runway that wasn't exactly Atlanta airport-sized, but one that he considered to be adequate, for refueling. He opted for the latter, fortunately, and those mud-flap gizmos on the wings did their job flawlessly as we roared in for a perfect landing and a proper stop.

So we ended up touching down in Atlanta a bit later than we had counted on, but none the worse for wear.

Atlanta itself is loaded with all the attractions–and headaches–of big cities everywhere, of course. But I also detected an ugly discrimination there–one that I have never seen any newspaper editorialize on or any TV talking head confront. It involves the letter "u" when it is engraved in stone on buildings.

I've seen this prejudice in places other than Atlanta, to be sure, but it seems to be particularly pervasive there. I saw several blatant examples, and jotted down a couple. For example, there was the First Chvrch of Christ, Scientist. And the DeKalb Covnty Covrt Hovse.

The argument, I'm sure, is that the guy with the hammer and chisel found it easier to make a "v" instead of a "u" and I can sympathize with that. But he didn't have any problem rounding off those "s's" and "d's" and "c's", so that argument simply doesn't hold water.

Also, you won't find it happening here in our county, because the "u's" engraved on the Yavapai County Court House are as round as a baby's bottom. You can check it out and see for yourself.

So we can thank our county's forefathers for their foresight in eliminating such typos before they were . . . well . . . in stone.

Prescott Courier, August 1999

PREACHER PURVEYS PLETHORA OF PRECEPTS IN POOH PARABLES

I feel no compunction about blaming Pastor Peter for the way he peppered the parishioners in the pews from the pulpit as he painted a painstaking picture of palatable palaver.

Some columns should carry warning labels right up front and this is one of them, because you might consider it to be reeking in fatuousness.

And, because of that and also the fact that shirking responsibility for actions a person isn't particularly proud of has become the American way of life lately. I'd like to place the blame on somebody else–Pastor Peter Perry, of all people, who is senior minister of the Prescott United Methodist Church.

It was Pastor Peter who came up with a sermon series on the various characters in "Winnie the Pooh", you see, and he topped it off with a sermon titled "Confronting Our Fears with Piglet and Pooh".

He'd earlier had some very nice things to say, incidentally, about the gang of characters ranging from Tigger to Eeyore to Piglet and, of course, Pooh. (After all, Pastor Peter would never be one to pooh-pooh Pooh–not in a hundred years. It's simply not his nature.)

Anyway, he told about an aunt of his who collects pigs (she's a swinophile, or oinkologist, as he so delicately put it), and he pointed out that over the years she has amassed an impressive collection of pigs–"Porky pigs, petunia pigs, porcelain pigs, pewter pigs, plastic pigs, pig platters, pig pillows."

All of that sets the stage for the following bit of nonsense, which I feel no compunction about in blaming on Pastor Peter for the way he peppered the parishioners in the pews from the pulpit as he painted a painstaking picture of palatable palaver.

Pertaining to Piglet, and to paraphrase, Pastor Peter portrayed the plump, pink, pudgy, pint-sized peewee porker as a paragon of plaintive paranoia whose principal predilection provided a palpable, yet poignant, penchant for passivity.

It's probably problematical, but Piglet's proclivity for peril produced peccadilloes that precluded any perceived push for panache.

But enough already! And please pardon me for lapsing into platitudinous and perfunctory perambulations. Getting to the meat of the subject, what Pastor Peter really said was that Piglet "is afraid of the unknown and the imagined" and that, much like that little guy, "our fears are often more imagined than real."

More often than not, though, he continued, "our greatest fears are reserved for those things that go bump in the night, the monster under the bed or in the closet, the eventuality that never happens."

51

And he quoted a letter written by John (he didn't provide a last name, but he's the John who follows right after Matthew, Mark and Luke in the Holy Bible) that ranks right up there on the wisdom scale:

"There is no fear in love, but perfect love casts out fear; for fear has to do with punishment, and whoever fears has not reached perfection in love."

Words to live by, wouldn't you say?

Prescott Courier, July 1999

ALL IS JUST DUCKY IN PALESTINE, EVEN ON STAGE

Her illness was so severe that she thought for sure that she was going to die, then that she WASN'T going to die. But Shirley, who of course is white, is now back in the pink after being blue.

I was in Palestine last week visiting my sister Shirley and her husband Ed. (Not THAT Palestine, you sillies! This one is in the green state of Texas, which is getting all the rain that we're not getting around here nowadays. My only fear is that if they succeed in seceding back there that they'll take their rainfall with

I'm happy to report that after suffering a major health hit that she thought for sure that she she WASN'T going to die. But now back in the pink after being part of her successful survival at the Rev. Roy Duncan, who is

What you must understand Bible Beltism. Remember when stations on just about every corner? a lot of corners instead, and Rev. (A super guy, by the way, who drive a school bus, who travels to pastors in support of children doesn't accompany him on the have Wal-Marts there"–and who Year.)

Anyway, when Shirley hit Roy asked his congregants to

Sister Shirley managed to fend off Grim Reaper

them and leave us high and dry.) Shirley is getting along fine now last month. Her illness was so severe was going to die, and then that Shirley, who of course is white, is blue. And I'd like to place at least the feet of her next-door neighbor, black.

going in is that Palestine is big in the nation had S&Ls or filling Well, in Palestine it's churches on Roy pastors a Baptist flock there. gets up at 5:30 weekday morns to Africa annually with some fellow there–his delightful wife Yvonne trips because, she quips, "they don't is Palestine's reigning Citizen of the

bottom health-wise, she told me, pray for the recovery of "our sister

Shirley." After all, she said he said that "she thinks I'm good-looking and resemble Sidney Poitier" and as such that she is definitely deserving of survival and maybe even redemption. (There's no way to know whether he blushed when he uttered that Poitier reference, based on his dark complexion, so I can only assume that he did.) Well, the congregants did (pray, that is), and Shirley did (recover, that is), so the Good Lord apparently responded positively to their entreaty.

So much for Shirley, and let's turn now to her husband, who is one of the most remarkable people of my experience. Ed Hiser is the type of guy who is knowledgeable in all things mechanical, electrical and technical–he's been a prime mover in the construction of power plants, nuclear and otherwise, for example. And if something is broke, he knows WHY it's broke and how to fix it.

Something of a new challenge presented itself to Ed last October, though, when high school drama students put out a call to recruit some adult townspeople for roles in a railroad-related production. (Palestine is a major East Texas rail center, with 27 lines having snaked into the town at one time.)

The "stage" for the planned play was a string of passenger cars that ended up accommodating more than 500 people who paid $65 apiece for a steak dinner and the privilege of riding in the rolling theater round-trip to Rusk while trying to solve the mystery posed by the play's title of "Murder on the Disorient Express". (Frankly, they got downright frisky with Agatha Christie because Rusk–which no doubt has charms–still doesn't measure up exotic-wise to, say, Istanbul or Calcutta, but what the hey?)

Now, getting back to my brother-in-law, Ed, who responded to the casting call by volunteering to serve as a newspaper reporter. This was totally foreign to him, but he agreed to do it and labored under the pseudonym of Buck Boyd with the Palestine Herald-Press. He even printed up business cards for legitimacy. In addition to the murder angle, a subplot related to a diamond heist, and Ed ended up interviewing passengers during stops along the way–which included the sighting of hippies (the targeted era was circa 1969), farmers and farmers' wives, and some space aliens decked out in tinfoil outfits and antennas, all of whom were flitting about in the deep woods of Anderson County–as the passengers strove to solve the mystery of the miscreant.

And you'll no doubt be surprised to learn who the murderer was. It was an FBI guy! After all, the vast majority of FBI agents simply aren't into that sort of thing, and I doubt that hardly any of the passengers on the Disorient Express fingered him as the bad guy. It was just so *out of character*, if you know what I mean.

Prescott Courier, May 2009

DEBATE HUMS ALONG ABOUT WHETHER BIRD HAS TONGUE

Frank Finley poses proudly in his Thank God I'm Frank shirt.

Bob also volunteered that they're the only birds that can fly backward. Fancy that! A bird with a reverse gear!

I do believe that somebody's been flying over the cuckoo's nest again on this hummingbird business.

Bill and Cassie Breeden were visiting Frank and Kay Finley a while back at the Finleys' Prescott home, and the four of them were shooting the breeze out on the back deck when a hummingbird began feeding at the feeder. Everyone was marveling at how well the bird was doing, and Cassie and Kay were really impressed that the little guy was managing to pull it off without benefit of a tongue.

This prompted guffaws from the two guys, both of whom are pro-tongue when it comes to hummingbirds, and Frank chided the ladies with; "Then what do they do . . . use their beaks as straws?"

Now I don't know about Bill—only that he rebuilt and installed the engine in Frank's '64 Ranchero and is helping out with the restoration—but I *do* know Frank and his myriad of problems, not the least of which is his penchant for extreme exaggeration.

So I donned my investigative reporter's hat to seek out a credible source on the subject: Sheila and Bob Murray of Wild Birds Unlimited over at the Depot Marketplace.

Yes, Sheila confirmed, those little hummers definitely have tongues that they can flick out way longer than their inch-and-a-half-long beaks and they "lap the nectar, just like a dog." Bob chimed in that their tongues are forked, too, which is irrelevant since they don't speak.

Bob also volunteered that they're the only birds that can fly backward. Fancy that! A bird with a reverse gear! . . . that they are indeed a rare bird because they can't walk ("don't need to," he said, "because they're never on the ground") . . . that the whirring noise you hear when they're around stems from 80 wing beats per second . . . and that they move out at 50 mph, give or take.

The Murrays also offered up a tidbit from the Arizona-Sonora Desert Museum's book on "The Secret Lives of Hummingbirds," noting that ""if a man used energy at a hummingbird's rate, every day he would need to eat nearly 40 ten-pound sacks of potatoes or more than 1,000 quarter-pound hamburgers." Now, that's a lot of burgers, with or without the cheese.

Well, to make a short story long, Frank subsequently got a mysterious missile in the mail that had "THE DAILY COURIER" in bold type at the top, along with a headline proclaiming "Fire Dept. Rescues Hummingbird." It also had a nice sketch of a hummingbird with its tongue sticking out. The bird was resting on its little clawed feet, too, that appeared to be very walkable.

After checking around the newsroom, though, I confirmed that the correspondence definitely didn't originate here. Frank said, though, somewhat darkly, that he suspects that "it came from Cassie Breeden." And you know, he may very well be right.

Anyway, here's the story:

"Prescott firefighters answered a call to rescue a hummingbird that had stuck its tongue inside a hummingbird feeder late Saturday afternoon. Spokesman Buddy Breeden, with the Arizona Bird Watchers Association, speaks out on behalf of the hummingbird:

"This poor hummingbird flew down for its afternoon meal but unbeknownst to him the homeowner, Frank Finley, had let the feeder get too low, causing the bird to have to extend his tongue beyond its capacity. The tongue swelled from the over-extension, causing it to become stuck in the dried-up opening of the feeder. The homeowners became aware of this situation after hearing a loud ruckus out on their deck, where they observed this terrible scene. They immediately called 911.

"There was no alternative but to break the feeder so paramedics could lubricate the hummingbird's tongue with a Dri Wash 'n' Guard product Mr. Finley had in his garage, freeing the bird immediately.

"After close inspection by the paramedics and firefighters at the scene, they determined that this disaster resulted in part from the homeowner's negligence. They did not cite Mr. Finley but warned him that if this incident were ever to reoccur they would fine him buckets of money."

During an interview with Mr. Finley, he told reporters, "I just don't have time to keep that damn thing full. I'm a very busy man, I own a '64 Ranchero, and I'm getting ready to open a Speed Shop."

Prescott Courier, undated, late 1990s

STREETWISE . . . AND FANCY-FREE

Some, I feel reasonably sure, would fantasize at the mere mention of Barbee Way,
Bikini Court and Coed Lane.

Instead of the name of the game, which is a tired cliché, let's call it the game of the name.

Happened to be browsing through Thomas Bros. Maps' Popular Street Atlas for Sacramento County last week (I know what you're thinking: Doesn't that guy have anything *better* to do with his time?), and ran across a batch of catchy references.

For example, if you're into the court system, let it be stated for the record that there is indeed a Law Court in Sacramento County and, if that's not appealing enough, there's always Appellate Court. Bailiff Way should help to keep things in order. There's also a Baptist Court, which I hadn't realized they had one of all to themselves.

Please don't consider me "racist" when I point out that there's a Triple Crown Court and an Arcaro Court jockeying for position in the atlas, plus what appears to be a choice of several steeds including Bold Ruler Way, Determined Court and Affirmed Way.

The flavor of the Old West is alive and well within the city and county, as witnessed to by such handles as: Cattle Drive, Covered Wagon Court, Hobble Court, Bunkhouse Way, Hideout Court, Cayuse Way, Warhorse Court, Stagecoach Drive, Stampede Court, Chuckwagon Drive, Compadre Court, Sourdough Court, Stage Line Court, Bullion Drive, Papoose Court, Cowcatcher Way, Crazy Horse Road, Paydirt Court, Horseshoe Drive and Roundup Court. Also Susanna Court, which there apparently has been a cry for.

Some, I feel reasonably sure, would fantasize at the mere mention of Barbee Way, Bikini Court and Coed Lane.

And believe it or not, there *is* a Ripley Street.

Biblically speaking, the offerings include Noah Court, Ark Way and Ararat Court.

Many of the names are catchy/cutesy, so plodding right along we have: Pedestrian Lane, Sunday Drive, Pretty Girl Court, Burnt Creek Way (huh?), Attaway Avenue, Bummer Street, Cackler Lane, Pivot Court, Divot Circle, Parody Way, Coot Alley, Milky Way, Poverty Road, Be Lazy Court, Merrily Way, Pixie Court, Teneight Way, Oaken Bucket Court, Green Eyes Way, Lucky Lindy Court, Butterball Way, Three Sisters Court, Cadjew Avenue (Gesundheit!), Running Water Court, Charbono (not Cherbono) Way, Torchy Court, Shovelers Lane and Fast Water Court.

Some are hard to say without taking a breath, such as Roseville's All America City Boulevard and Folsom's American River Canyon Drive, whereas others are short and snappy: Up Court, The Court, In Court, Jo Court and Mi Court.

Still others are melodious or whimsical, examples being: Sunmist Way, Pinafore Court, Summer Rain Way, Candy Cove Court, Waxwing Way, Whisperwillow Drive, Chantilly Lane (not Lace), Fairytale Street, Blarney Court, Anice Street, Sudden Wind Court, Folklore Way, Irish Mist Way, Lamplighter Lane, Glass Slipper Way and Witchinghour Court.

Among my all-time favorites, though, are some of the "way" streets. For starters, we would trot out Tay Way, Gay Way and Jay Way. To say nothing of Pollen Way (a natural to do with Cadjew Avenue, but alas! One is in the North Area and the other is a Southerner), Any Way and Harms Way (which I've always been told to stay out of the way of).

Last, but not least, there's a Goinyour Way. (Just so you'll know, I tried to find an Ididitmy Way, but failed.)

Sacramento Bee, undated, early 1980s

MOBILIZING FOR THE "MOBILES"

Let's put it this way: have you ever known a mobile home inhabitant who called his place a trailer? Probably not.

A Harley-Davidson is not a scooter.
The Queen Mary is not a skiff.
And, a mobile home is not a trailer.

That last little truism needs an explanation. Why? Well, it's because the mobile home industry has this image problem that surfaces on occasion. Too often, such units are referred to as "trailers"–a term that, at least in my estimation, is out of touch with reality.

Let's put it this way: Have you ever known a mobile home inhabitant who called his place a trailer? Probably not. The word comes down sort of hard on the ear when you're talking about a place to live. And another reminder: mobile homes nowadays aren't all that mobile. Ever tried to tow one behind your jitney? Don't.

In my zeal to right what I consider to be a wrong, I consulted the dictionary, knowing full well that such a perusal could only serve to bolster my case. Sad to say, it didn't. Here's how the definition for mobile home reads: "A large trailer outfitted as a home meant to be parked more or less permanently at a location." Aaargh!

And then, to add insult to injury, was this definition for *trailerite,* of all things: "A person living in a mobile home." Now, *that* smarted. Webster really knows how to hurt a guy, huh?

What brought on this whole ridiculous exercise was a quiet little paragraph in a wire service story of a few days ago that had to do with a drop in the FHA-VA interest rate. "The new rate for an FHA mobile home loan," the article concluded, "is down half a point to 14 percent, or 13.5 percent if purchase of a parking spot is included."

That "parking spot" grated greatly, I must admit, in that it conjured up the image of someone driving around with his house hitched behind, diligently searching for a place to park the thing. (A meter maid hanging a ticket on the front doorknob is a terrifying thought, too, believe you me.)

Ah, well. Call 'em what you will, but mobile homes are definitely here to stay. There are now parking places (oops!) on permanent foundations (which makes them "manufactured" instead of "mobile" homes in FHA's estimation) . . . FHA is filling a need by offering 30-year loan insurance on such manufactured units . . . design and construction is such that many mobile/manufactured homes are hard to distinguish from their conventionally "stick built" cousins . . . their pricing is attractive . . . zoning restrictions are being eased . . . and they're constructed according to a HUD-established national building code.

By: Jerry W. "Slats" Jackson

And so it is, notes Ted Eggering, president of the San Francisco-based International Organization of Real Estate Appraisers, that "little by little, the image, land-use and financing impediments that have so inhibited the growth of this industry are being eliminated. Simply stated, manufactured housing has come of age."

Sacramento Bee, September 1982

IT'S SAFETY FIRST—AND LAST—WITH THIS GREY EAGLE

"While flying with piston-type aircraft, engine failures were fairly commonplace. But during those years of jet flying with American, I was never confronted with a single engine failure."
—Durward "Duke" Ledbetter

You hear about it off and on.

Horatio Q. Success—budding steel executive; fortyish; graying slightly at the temples; off in search of his second million; a tough nut to crack across the bargaining table; enjoys that before-dinner nip and after-dinner nap; charming wife and a son who managed to crack the Yale barrier.

$uch a $ucce$$, in fact, that he couldn't resist the temptation of heeding those ads geared for a man of his means.

Horatio, you see, has joined the ballooning ranks of flying executives. He's a go-go-getter and potential jet-setter.

He's also the proud owner of a sleek new Beech Bonanza. Red with white trim, wall-to-wall carpeting, and even a bar. A modest one, of course, which is the only modest thing there is about Horatio.

After all, he's logged almost 200 hours of time since he went on this flying kick, and there doesn't appear to be anything worth knowing when it comes to piloting planes that he doesn't already know.

His horizons, you might say, are unlimited.

It all sounded great until you picked up the afternoon paper and took a casual gander at the headline proclaiming "Steel Magnate, Three Others, Die in Crash".

"When are they going to start making foolproof planes?" you mumble to yourself as your abbreviated attention span goes in quest of Barney Google and Snuffy Smith.

What you *didn't* know, though, is that poor Horatio had had a couple of martinis before his final joyride. He prided himself in being able to hold his liquor and didn't stop to consider that two martinis at sea level pack a four-martini wallop at 7,000 feet.

Flight plans are for novices, too, he'd joked to his friends as he sauntered over to his Beech in true John Wayne fashion and clamped on the headset with a carefree flourish. So, how were they to know it was the kid's last flight?

With Lady Luck by his side, Horatio was airborne. As an afterthought, he waggled his wings at the boys in the tower in an A-OK overture smacking of no small amount of bravura.

Mr. Success cruised around for a while in the blue, pointing out areas of interest to the three admiring friends, then nonchalantly pulled back on the controls with a "think I'll take 'er up to 10 thousand."

What he didn't know, though, was that there was this big jetliner which was already well into its landing pattern up ahead.

Granted, the bigger bird was a good two miles away when Horatio got caught in its wake. The Beech was turned inside-out, though, and—according to the newspaper account—bits of wreckage and people were found scattered over an area a half-mile square.

What Mr. Success had failed to take into account, you see, were those air whirlpools (vortices) swirling off the wing tips of that 707 as it roared along at a 500 mile per hour clip. Run a finger quickly through a tub of bath water, and you'll get the idea. The whirlpool of water created by the gesture materializes in the same manner that miniature tornadoes do off a jet's hurrying wing tips.

It was a lesson that Horatio didn't have much time to take to heart.

Durward "Duke" Ledbetter knows about such things, though, and is doing his level-best to get the word out on flight safety to anyone who will listen. Formerly of Redwood City, Calif., he is now a Prescott resident and a man eminently qualified to expound on the virtues of safety in flight.

Ledbetter gave up piloting airliners 18 months ago—it's mandatory at age 60, you know—and is presently in the midst of an undying safety crusade that should bring results.

As an American Airlines pilot, the veteran flyer has posted a phenomenal record during a career that has seen him log over 12 million miles commercially while in the airways some 33,000 hours. My slide rule verifies that as being over three and a half *years* among the clouds.

Over that span, he has transported around 550,000 passengers safely to their destinations. Not only that, but he still holds two commercial speed records that were set late in his 35-year career with American Airlines.

One of the marks was established in a Boeing 707 Astrojet on a hop from New York to San Francisco—he averaged 554.88 miles per hour on that particular swing—whereas the other gained him international acclaim when he piloted a Boeing 720 from Chicago to Mexico City in the space of three hours and 10 minutes.

Most of his reminders are necessarily grim:

"About one-third of the (private plane) crashes involve drinking by the pilot prior to the flight."

"Ninety-eight percent of the accidents can be traced to pilot error or deficiency."

"In my experience, the most dangerous pilot I've found is the successful businessman who has made enough money to buy a plane, has learned to fly, and has accumulated a few hundred hours of flying time. It's difficult for them to believe it (flying) is a specialized operation. You just can't operate a plane in the same manner you do a business."

"An outstanding error is attempting to fly through weather beyond the limitations of the craft."

"A pilot is no better than the instruments he has to rely on."

Special stress is placed on the menace of liquor, which has no place in the cockpit. Any commercial pilot caught drinking while on duty or within 24 hours prior to flying is dismissed on the spot, the veteran pilot explains, and there is no recourse whatsoever. The rule holds true with entire crews, he adds, as all hands must be on their toes in order to cope with any emergency that may arise.

What of jets as opposed to conventional prop jobs?

He's sold on the big ones.

"While flying with piston-type aircraft, engine failures were fairly commonplace. But during those years of jet flying with American, I was never confronted with a single engine failure."

Ledbetter is settling down to a not-so-hectic mode of life at present with his attractive wife, Catherine, in their new west Prescott dwelling. She was one of the first stewardesses to fly with United Airlines back in the days when one of the requirements for the job was that applicants be registered nurses.

Meanwhile, the longtime flyer, who is serving as national president of the Grey Eagles Association—an organization of veteran American Airlines pilots—has naturally witnessed hordes of changes since helping to pioneer commercial aviation.

He learned to fly in a famed "Jenny" aircraft in Kansas City during the year 1923. With 90 horses under the cowling, the World War I bi-plane served him well as a trainer.

During the war that came along after "the war to end all wars," he served in the Air Corps from a South Pacific vantage point, with duties centered around hospital evacuation via DC4s and C-54s.

Ledbetter comes by his safety-consciousness honestly. The year was 1924 when he saw a plane crack up right in the big middle of a Kansas City street. The barnstorming pilot was killed and his cargo of hundreds of leaflets scattered to the four winds.

"Flying is safe if conducted properly" was the simple message emblazoned on the leaflets.

His impression of the incident was, to say the least, an indelible one.

"I still have to keep an open mind," the bronzed airways veteran mused as he speculated on the day-to-day advances in the rarefied realm of air transportation. "The minute I think I know it all is when I become a menace to myself and everyone who happens to be with me."

To have had his head in the clouds so long, Mr. Ledbetter has done a remarkable job of keeping his feet on the ground.

Prescott Courier, September 1965

IT'S A TOWN HAUNTED BY GHOSTS

The concentration camp located near the outskirts of Dachau is an open wound that has been left open for all to see.

Dachau, a quiet village located near metropolitan Munich, has a name to live down. For it was there that Nazi Germany reached its depth of degradation by slaughtering thousands upon thousands of victims whose only crime was being born in the wrong place.

The concentration camp located near the outskirts of Dachau is an open wound that has been left open for all to see. The rows upon rows of shacks that once held the unfortunates are still there. And–in the main compound, now peaceful with only the soundlessness of grass and flowers growing–the ovens remain.

Floral wreaths decorate those ovens now. The flowers lend a strange incoherency to what is now and what was then.

Mute testimony in remembrance of what the camp once was has not been covered up or even glossed over to any extent. Through efforts of the Allies, it has been preserved as a stark memorial to the lengths to which man's inhumanity to man can sink.

Outside the compound, a large monument to Dachau's dead has been erected. It is silo-shaped, with a portion of its side carved out to reveal the memorial housed inside. Topping it is a modernistic tangle of twisted steel rods giving the illusion of a crown of thorns.

Except for plaques explaining otherwise, the compound grounds resemble an immaculately-kept park. Within the shady lanes and on the ivy-covered walls are reminders of the era that must never be duplicated again. A large wooden box on stilted legs that held the ashes of unknown innocents . . . a gleaming white monument crested by a carved Star of David guarding a now-flowered grave of countless hundreds . . . the pistol range where defenseless souls were murdered at point-blank range . . . a gallows site . . .

They're all there, blandly described in German, French and English inscriptions.

Inside the main building are posted remembrances–in blown-up photos and statistical charts–of the camp's operation. The first photograph to be seen on entering is about five feet wide and four feet deep. It depicts Hitler and several of his lieutenants at the height of the Nazi heyday.

In all of Germany, it was the only picture I saw of the former fuehrer and, I might add, it was a not-too-good likeness of him. You see, his eyes had been carved out by someone–at some time–who must have remembered too well.

Brownfield News-Herald, July 1964

SAVE PETROL, TYRES; TAKE THE TUBE!

It is rumored that the topless bathing suit is being introduced to England just so you can once again tell the girls from the boys.

To have learned the language first, the British haven't had much success in doing just a whole lot with it. They persist on driving on the wrong side of the street, too.

Many of their expressions I'm sure you're familiar with. Things like referring to gasoline as "petrol". Our 'tire' is their "tyre", of course. And they don't travel to work in London on a subway. 'Tis a "tube" instead.

Another example popped out at me as I was glancing over an issue of the *London Daily Mail* while over on that side of the pond recently. The article was telling of a man of TV and radio fame who had been assailed by another man while riding on a train. "I had dozed off," the personality related, "when suddenly I felt my head being thumped . . ."

It all came back to me again when I phoned the Pan Am office to confirm flight reservations back to this part of the world. "Just bring your tickets right in," the very Britishy voice on the other end articulated, "and we'll tidy 'um right up for ye."

While in the sprawling city of London, Pat and I visited with my father's cousin and family. He's a naval commander serving a tour of duty there, with their living quarters being situated in a suburb spelled Ruislip and pronounced RYE-slip. A very charming family, and—with two teenaged sons and a teen daughter–there's never a dull moment to rear its head.

During a typically rainy afternoon, we hopped a guided tour bus of the city for a look at some of the historical spots to be found there. Although almost 20 years after the Great Conflict, some war scars still are to be seen. All of which makes for occasional gaping holes in the skyline, but those are being slowly but methodically filled in by modern new structures.

Our tour guide bore a striking resemblance to Richard Burton. It couldn't have been him, though, since he was Liz-less at the time. He carried on an interesting commentary regarding the various sights we were viewing. For instance, in regard to the building housing the realm's vital statistics–i.e., births, marriages and deaths–he observed that, "Here we have the Hatched, Matched and Detached Bureau."

We–and every other tourist-type not over at Stratford helping Bill Shakespeare celebrate his 400th birthday–naturally felt compelled to witness the changing of the guard while in London. A band added to the pomp and circumstance of the occasion, its members dolled up in bright red jackets, black trousers, and the inevitable high furry hats. Looked a lot like a (Texas) Tech marching band staffed with only drum majors, and we were more than a little surprised when they strode past playing one of Tech's marching songs. It smacked of plagiarism, but I kept the silence on the theory that we should let Her Majesty have her fun and also that there's the chance–a slim one, of course–that Tech might've swiped the ditty from the British. After all, there were a lot of "Red Raiders" at the Boston Tea Party.

We saw some Mods and Rockers while over there. For any adult who might not be familiar with the terms, any teenager can tell you that a Mod is a young man who dons lipstick, rouge and the like and wears frilly clothes, whereas a Rocker is one of the rival mob typified by motorcycles and leather jacket attire. The Rockers are fundamentally tougher–pound for pound–compared to the Mods, but the Mods pitifully outnumber them. As a consequence, the rumbles are fairly evenly matched and a lot more interesting from a spectator standpoint.

The Beatle influence is visibly evident in London, where many of the men can be seen parading around with flowing locks all the way down to their shoulder blades. It is rumored that the topless bathing suit is being introduced to England just so you can once again tell the girls from the boys, in fact.

But seriously, it *is* a problem of some magnitude, since all who wear tresses don't necessarily wear dresses. Many young people one spots on London streets nowadays leave bona fide doubt as to whether they be male or female.

Only their hairdressers know for sure.

Brownfield News-Herald, July 1964

Oh, What Is So Rare as a Fondue in Heidelberg?

"Jerry, let's face it. You'll never be anything but a beanstick."
—Siglinde Whitson

World War II fortunately bypassed historic old Heidelberg, the ancient university city that is nestled comfortably astraddle the lazy Neckar River deep in the heart of West Germany.

It was there that the spouse and I enjoyed a visit with the Whitsons–Bob and Siglinde–for a brief while a few weeks ago.

The get-together was something of a reunion for Bob and me, as we had been stationed together over there in '57. Upon his release from Uncle Sam's care he married Siglinde, a charming and lively German girl, and the two of them settled down in Heidelberg. At present, Bob is associated with a sporting goods concern, and travels over much of Europe in his line of work.

It was at the Whitsons' home that we got ourselves initiated into the Order of the Fondue.

A fondue, in case you don't happen to be familiar with the term, is sort of a do-it-yourself meat entrée. Any of you housewives who haven't tried it might lend an ear, as the preparation is a real dilly.

From an artillery angle, the hostess furnished each of us with a long, skinny fork. Next, she placed a boiling hot container of cooking oil in the middle of the table, supplemented with candles beneath it to keep it bubbling. The meat itself was cubed roast beef–about two inches square–and totally raw. All we guests had to do was to spear the little chunks, plop them into the oil, and in a matter of about eight sizzling seconds we had for ourselves a delightful delicacy on the end of our individual forks.

It all made for a highly entertaining meal, to say the least, and never once did the conversation threaten to lag.

Siglinde is a delightful sprite-like person, incidentally. Her elfin personality is only enhanced by a minor difficulty with the English language. Being of German descent, she naturally has trouble pronouncing certain of our sounds and incorporating certain expressions, just as we Americans find it impossible to attain the guttural sound characteristic of the German tongue or the uppity accent that is such a favorite of our good British forefathers.

During one animated conversation she explained that her little girl had been "running forth and back" all morning, for instance.

Her primary problem is centered around the pesky "th" sound, however. All of which explains her astute observation of "Patsy, don't you ever feed Jerry? After all, he's so *sin!*"

"Sank you," I injected in playful rebuttal, and she came back at me with a distinct air of resignation by sighing, "Jerry, let's face it. You'll never be anything but a beanstick."

Can life continue to be worth living after hearing such a glum prediction?

Brownfield News-Herald, July 1964

THE NAME SOUNDS FAMILIAR, BUT . . .

I fully expected to see scads of Hitlerian relics at Eagle's Nest, which is now used as a restaurant. On the contrary, though, there was not so much as one swastika or Maltese Cross to be found in the whole works. Not even a sign saying "Adolf slept here."

Adolf Hitler, a fascist fanatic who demanded–and got–a fanatical following from among the German people, is practically a forgotten man in his homeland now. The individual who personally launched millions upon millions of miseries against mankind is no longer the apple of the modern German's eye.

This fact was evidenced repeatedly while my wife Pat and I were touring parts of Germany last month, and was made particularly crystal-clear on a morning tour to Eagle's Nest, which served as Hitler's mountaintop hangout during his lush years when dreams of world conquest seemed to be no more than a goosestep away.

An elaborate dwelling perched on the very top of the world, it overlooks Berchtesgaden, a recreation area just across the border from Salzburg, Austria. It also peers down on the Konigsee, which has to be the most beautiful lake in all of creation. Its waters are the greenest, cleanest and serenest imaginable. So green, in fact, that it looks like paint. 'Cept it ain't.

After chugging up the narrow Pikes Peaky road by bus (they don't allow cars to make the trip), we were dropped off above the timberline and within about a hundred yards of Eagle's Nest–straight up. From there we had the option of hopping an elevator following a short walk through a tunnel or walking the distance by means of an asphalted hairpin trail.

We chose the elevator, which turned out to be the fanciest ever. Its interior was enormous and constructed of shiny brass that sparkled like gold. It was also heated (only a 10-secoind ride from bottom to top, but nothing was too good for the fuehrer!) and had padded seats around three of its sides that would accommodate about 20 people.

I fully expected to see scads of Hitlerian relics at Eagle's Nest, which is now used as a restaurant. On the contrary, though, there was not so much as one swastika or Maltese Cross to be found in the whole works. Not even a sign saying "Adolf slept here." It was totally devoid of any recollection of the onetime Nazi leader.

Germany, you see, has successfully striven to cleanse itself of his memory. He is now no more than a bad dream that has been put to rest, although up until his suicide death in a Berlin bunker the German people as a whole continued to look to him as their salvation. It's a weird transition they've accomplished, but appears to be a sincere about-face.

The turning of an entire populace's back on its former fallen idol can be a subtle thing or a starkly overt one. This fact was apparent in the former instance by the lack of even a reference to his name within the halls of Eagle's Nest and in the latter by an object that has been erected beside the footpath leading down from the building.

The object, which would have been reviled and belittled by the Little Caesar during his lifetime, is in the form of a 10-foot cross that stands guard over the valley that is Berchtesgaden's.

A cross of Calvary and the vision of Hitler are as incoherent as a concoction made up of ice cream and sauerkraut. It would seem to prove one thing, though–West Germany appears to be leaning in the right direction.

Brownfield News-Herald, July 1964

CROWN KING: IT'S A WHOLE OTHER WORLD

Dick will tell you that at one time there were about a dozen taverns gracing the area between Crown King proper and the Crown King Mine. . . .A thirst of the sluice sleuths was apparently not for gold alone.

Chug southward from Prescott along the blacktopped Black Canyon Highway.

Tributarily lost in your wake is the Big Bug Trickle–a lazy stream with no visions whatsoever of river grandeur. Content, rather, to zigzag this way and that, incessantly necessitating the building of little bridges to span its wanderings.

Don't miss that gentle right at the Junction called Cordes. It's the turn that takes you to the land of Phoenix–Birdburg beneath the sun.

A mere three miles past the Cordes Junction juncture is a sign promising that Crown King and the Horse Thief Recreation Road are that way. It is at this point that you steer right again, this time onto a trusty but dusty road pointed generally toward the Bradshaws, by now thinly veiled in a foreboding blanket of mist blue.

The road is an interesting one.

On your left downstairs is a batch of beehives, the honeyed hutches abuzz.

A barn that every artist would love to sketch commands the terrain at tiny Cordes.

Driving further, you come onto juniper dotting the hillsides, along with the perennial prickly pear and occasional saguaro. Skinny sentinels in the form of telephone poles stand watch.

Just before coming to Cleator you enter Prescott National Forest. Cleator's ocotillo atmosphere offers a temporary respite to the traveler, who is invited to stop at "The" Mecca (not to be confused with any other Mecca). It's there that you can drop in for "homemade pie & stuff".

The terrain becomes progressively rugged. On the right hand and on the left you are reminded that you're deep in the heart of mining territory. Signs tell the story and point the general direction. Signs such as Blue Bell . . . Silver Christmas . . . Zeno . . . Howard Silver . . . Swastika . . . Goat Ranch . . . Algonquin Trail . . . Hell's Hole.

Your pulse quickens as you traverse a gorge and find yourself in the big little middle of pine-populated Crown King.

Something in excess of 25 people call Crown King home. A one-room school–grades one through eight–stands as the edifice of educational edification.

Dick and Jean Wheaton tend to the store and post office. The sign on the outskirts of town had earlier assured you that the Crown King Store is "preferred by 5 out of every 4 people," and the Wheatons are living evidence of the reasons why.

Dick will tell you that at one time there were about a dozen taverns gracing the area between Crown King proper and the Crown King Mine. (The two are less than a mile apart.) A thirst of the sluice sleuths was apparently not for gold alone.

A decent rock-thrower can heave a stone from the post office to the site of the only remaining tavern still in existence. Grant Van Tilborg is proprietor there. He looks and acts a lot like Will Rogers, and rolls his own. Grant has had the place for about 10 years, and it's the most typically typical tavern you've ever witnessed.

All manner of yesteryear trappings adorn the walls. Like, for instance, a copper 1932 Arizona license plate. "There were more of those on the roads than on cars," Grant recalls, referring to the way in which the plates were prone to vibrate loose from their moorings. Copper tags died a timely death after three years, he explains.

Then there's a sign over the tavern sanctum warning that "Trespassers will be violated". And a scribbled reminder on a yellowed envelope, cautioning you to "Remember, only forest fires can prevent bears".

Still another bit of sagely advice observes that, "Work is the curse of the drinking class".

Glance over your shoulder and you'll see pictures of the past, including the moment of truth in '04 when they had that double hanging in Prescott.

Crown King, you'll find, is steeped in perpetuity.

Prescott Courier, April 1966

THE ASPENS ARE QUAKING AT POTATO PATCH

Then there was Potato Patch's pig farmer. His squealers reluctantly furnished bacon, pork and pickled feet to an ever-hungry populace.

I can resist almost anything except temptation.

It is for that reason—and that reason only—that I chose last week to succumb to the overpowering urge, load the wee family into a certain two-toned hack, and head out on a junket to a beckoning Senator Highway hideout.

This particular parcel of paradise is called Potato Patch.

Potato Patch . . . named for a spud farmer whose nuggets all had eyes. Mining camps, like army camps, travel on their stomachs, and his was the task of supplying a community with the baked, boiled and mashed starches of life.

Then there was Potato Patch's pig farmer. His squealers reluctantly furnished bacon, pork and pickled feet to an ever-hungry populace.

A lead pipe juts up from the spot where his cabin once stood. Surrounding it is a crumbling foundation, protecting the one-eyed pipe that stares hollowly back at Time.

Mushrooms? If you're in the right season, you'll find an abundance of them in the area. They thrive on mountain air, too; or is it overactive thyroid glands? Some weighing as much as eight pounds have been extracted from the hills.

The most picturesque asset the area has to offer, though, is its aspens. Their quaking splendor is unparalleled.

Potato Patch is perched at 6,700 feet—within walking distance of Walker and running distance of Hassayampa Lake. Every path leading out from it has a mystery all its own, or so it would appear.

One trail, for instance, passes by a once-warm but now deserted cabin which looks like it might be on its last pilings. Both doors leading into the two-roomer were wide open, curiously inviting entrance past a peeling "No Trespassing" sign.

The interior was, in a word, cluttered. A smattering of cooking utensils lolled listlessly from nails above a battered cookstove. Rumpled bedding lay heaped atop twin metal beds. Magazines and playing cards were strewn about over a cracking layer of linoleum. The king of spades peered back at me from the corner of his eye with an expressionless stare, dolefully wishing for his queen of hearts.

A yellow and yellowing Reader's Digest ("21st Year of Publication, Articles of Lasting Interest") next caught my attention. It was June of 1942, and . . .

"On December 21, 1941, seven Japanese planes took off from Indo-China to raid the Kunming terminus of the Burma Road. They expected no difficulty. Had not the Rising Sun dominated the eastern skies for four years?

"Suddenly three pairs of planes appeared out of the clouds and swooped down on the Japs. In 20 seconds six of the raiders fell in flames. The frightened survivor, when he reached his base, could report little except that on the prow of each fighter plane was painted the head of a grinning, saber-toothed tiger shark."

And, I remembered Chennault.

The magazine's section devoted to picturesque speech and patter told me that "there'll be little change in men's pockets this year." It also quoted a timely car-sale advertisement to the effect that "Car is A-1, Owner is 1-A".

"Digesting" a little further, I found that "perhaps our chief individual enemy, next to Adolf Hitler, is leather-faced, bullet-headed, bitter-hearted Isoroku Yamamoto, Commander in Chief of the Japanese fleet, a man whose whole life has been dedicated to the crushing of white supremacy." It was at this point that I played a little game by inserting in the place of Yamamoto such monickers as Castro, Sukarno, Nasser, Mao Tse-Tung and various and sundry other sordid surnames. Each insertion sounded great, and there was little to choose from between them.

While still wrapped up in a pensive mood, I scanned the Digest's menu of that time and ran across articles entitled "This Summer—Watch Out For Ticks!" and "The People Are Ahead of Congress" ("Congress should forget the pressure groups and realize that the public is eager to make sacrifices . . .").

Nothing is eternal, you say? I would hasten to disagree, and suggest instead that everything around us possesses an incontestable touch of eternity.

Prescott Courier, June 1966

SOME REFLECTIONS ON BUCKEY ... AND ...

So, let New Orleans have its Mardi Gras and Munich its Fasching. Prescott has its Frontier Days–complete with colorful parade–and is tremendously proud of the fact.

Buckey's still a driving force within Prescott's proud and pulsating heart

It was 1888, as very few of us recall, and no doubt a vintage year in the rip–roaring life of Prescott, Arizona.

Buckey O'Neill, we speculate, was still busying himself with dipping enticing pigtails into inkwells, and . . .

How's that? You say you haven't met Buckey?

Well, actually, the name's Capt. William O. O'Neill, but we seriously doubt that he would have answered to such a handle. Among other activities, Buckey served as captain of the Prescott Grays, sort of a National Guardish outfit of the day. He also helped deal those upstart Spaniards some misery while Rough Riding with Teddy Roosevelt before–alas!–meeting an untimely end.

Buckey's still a driving force within the proud and pulsating Prescott heart, though. Ever since '07, for instance, he has been keeping watch–from beneath a bronzed brow–over the various goings-on in the vicinity of the Yavapai County Courthouse. From beneath that pinned-back brim of a San Juan Stetson, he casts a longing look across Gurley Street–straight through the Avenue of Flags.

Due west of Buckey's bandoliered left shoulder is an historic hunk of real property commonly referred to as Whiskey Row. "The Row" comes equipped with such landmarks as the Palace Bar . . . and more memories than the average cowboy can shake a spur at.

There are still those, for example, who recall that warm July night around the turn of the century when an unfriendly fire lapped up Whiskey Row, leaving nothing more than ashes and rubble.

Naturally, a tragedy of such magnitude set the community back on its collective haunches. But, not for long.

A tent town dubbed "Dawson City" sprouted mysteriously the following afternoon on the Courthouse Plaza, and the "fire water" was flowing once again–this time with an unmistakable alcoholic content.

Call it pioneering spirit, American ingenuity, or what you will, but that's how it happened. It's enough to give Carrie Nation a conniption.

Anyway, this is the kingdom that Buckey surveys from atop his stalwart steed as he guards the entrance to the county coffers. He's just about the most sacred hombre to be found around these parts . . . and a constant reminder of an era that is gone but can never be forgotten.

I seem to have strayed, however, from the magical '88 that prompted an impromptu flashback.

It was on July 4th that a colorful cowpoke known as Arizona Charlie threw (well, actually it was "throwed") and tied a steer in the sum total of 59 and a half seconds. This feat earned for him a silver buckle and, unwittingly, gave documentation in later years to Prescott's claim of having the world's oldest rodeo.

Oh, the claim has been disputed more than once, notably by residents of Payson in eastern Arizona. This particular form of western entertainment was originally theirs, they'll tell you.

Regardless of the "Paysonification," though, the Prescott populace will point out that it's mighty hard to argue with a bona fide belt buckle, and therein provides validity to the calculated contention.

Be that as it may, Prescott's Frontier Days celebration—a three-day rodeo extravaganza geared around the Fourth of July—has been observed each year since the '88 inauguration. The annual venture has enjoyed the fat years during that prolonged stretch . . . and has survived the lean ones.

So, let New Orleans have its Mardi Gras and Munich its Fasching. Prescott has its Frontier Days—complete with colorful parade—and is tremendously proud of the fact.

A modern-day cowboy just may be getting his hops from an all-aluminum can . . .

And a bronc buster who finished out of the money (Give 'im a hand, folks; that's all the pay he's gonna get!") may not find solace in the form of a painted pay-for-player in the dimly lit corridor of a rickety hotel . . .

Frontier Days visitors will have a good time of it, though.

Buckey'll see to that.

Prescott Courier, June 1967

"Unreal Estate" Defines It Nicely

The landscape is speckled with saguaro, each of which is curiously reaching with needled arms. Some are reaching for the sky. Others for their neighbors. Still others for the pure and simple sake of keeping up with the Saguaro Joneses.

Contrary to popular belief, that resort hotel down at Castle Hot Springs doesn't really exist at all. Following considerable speculation on the subject, you see, I've come to the studied conclusion that it's all one big mirage. After all, they just don't grow things quite like that in Yavapai County, Arizona . . .

The wife and three-year-old offspring accompanied me a while back into that secluded section of the world. Our mission, shrouded in a cloak of secrecy: To See What In The Devil's Down There.

As we hair-pinned it down off Yarnell Hill, we swapped the cool crispness of the pine country for the heavier atmosphere of the yucca-studded desert floor. Three double-dip ice cream cones later we had left Wickenburg gasping amid our exhaust fumes and were again motoring south. But not for long. It's a left turn at Morristown and onto a little dirt road whose primary problem is curvature of the spinal cord.

Getting there, they say, is half the fun. This is particularly true as it relates to the snaky bit of dust-bound hard surface. It's dizzying, but–interestingly enough–in varying degrees. The landscape is speckled with saguaro, each of which is curiously reaching with needled arms. Some are reaching for the sky. Others for their neighbors. Still others for the pure and simple sake of keeping up with the Saguaro Joneses.

All the while, you're gingerly playing footsy with the Maricopa County line. The midday heat, combined with the slinky caterpillar-ish terrain, finally get the best of you. Hint number one is when you round a bend and think you see a sign proclaiming the presence of one Castle Hot Springs Hotel. Ridiculous, you mumble, and the mirage broadens to take in what appears to be an elongated stable to starboard and a carefully manicured golf course to port.

Palm trees pepper this out-of-this-world oasis–this panorama that has to be joking.

Entranced by the magnitude of the mirage, you hurry on through the taunting heat waves toward a porticoed pastel palace–a shimmering sham complete with an Olympic-sized pool that isn't there, tennis courts that must be making believe, and imaginary yum-yum trees loaded to the gills with grapefruit.

Funny thing, but the whole handsome spectacle would be believable if we were in, say, Palm Springs. Or Palm Beach. Or Palma de Mallorca. This is Yavapai, though . . . Land of the delightful delirium and happy hallucinatory hunting grounds.

Prescott Courier, April 1966

WRITER'S "GRAMP" IS PROUD AS PUNCH OF FIONA

Fiona Jackson

"At 5 o'clock sharp (Fred was never late) Fred was ready. He was wearing a new tux and had on girls' perfume. (He thought it smelled better than cologne.)"
—Fiona Jackson

Note: *We're all familiar with Garrison Keillor's observation that "all the children are above average" in Lake Wobegon. But I'm here to say that my three grandkids are (blush!) way WAY above average. Emma, Fiona and Noah Jackson are their names, and following is a column that ran in the Prescott Courier on March 17, 2009. It focuses on one of a trilogy of essays that Fiona wrote as an 11-year-old.*

Wife Pat and I have this granddaughter in San Diego, Fiona Jackson, who is cute as a bug, sharp as a tack, and friendly as a huntin' dog. (The similes abound!) We drove over to the coast last week to help celebrate her 12th birthday, and while there our son Kerry shared with us a copy of "The Fred Chronicles," a trilogy of essays that Fiona composed last year. They're delightfully written and, I think, are suitable for sharing.

First, there is the word picture of the man: "Fred is short and fat. He has mousy brown hair. He is a very strange man. He washes and conditions his mustache *every* day. For such a strange man, Fred is very clean. He works at Wal-Mart. But he thinks he is a *very* famous movie star. That is how strange he is. Fred has a good sense of humor and is very honest. He lives with his pet myna bird. He talks to him all the time. Mr. Myna (for that was his name) called Fred 'Elmo' but Fred understood. Mr. Myna *loved* Sesame Street."

Our friend Fred, though, has a problem, in that he "is in love with his manager at Wal-Mart. But he does not think she likes him. He tries very hard to get her to like him by hugging her every chance he gets."

The hugging, it turns out, pays off handsomely, with the telltale hint being embodied in the title of the final trilogic segment: "Fred Gets Married."

Following is Fiona's rundown: "Fred was born in Tennessee and he still lives there today. As you already know, Fred works at Wal-Mart. He is deeply in love with his manager, Jamie. She is young and beautiful. Secretly, she deeply loves the not so young and not so beautiful Fred. (But) Fred thinks she doesn't even know his last name.

"One day, Fred approached her. He was going to hug her but decided against it. Instead, he blurted out, 'Do you want to go to the air freshener company with me??' Jamie did not really know what the air freshener company was but she wanted to go somewhere with Fred, so she agreed. Fred fainted. The poor boy had been expecting a *'no way!!'* When he came to, Jamie said, 'See you at 5. Oh, and *get back to work.'*

"Fred had actually wanted to ask Jamie to come to a nice Greek restaurant but was blinded by her beauty and his mind went blank except for the air freshener company. Fred loved the air freshener company for two reasons. One, it smelled really good there, and two, his obsessive compulsive friend Bob worked there.

"At 5 o'clock sharp (Fred was never late) Fred was ready. He was wearing a new tux and had on girls' perfume. (He thought it smelled better than cologne.) As they were on their way to the air freshener company, Fred asked Jamie if she would like to go out to dinner at a Greek restaurant. She said absolutely. They had a very romantic night.

"Two years later Jamie and Fred were still going out. That night Fred had asked Jamie to marry him. He gave her a really pretty diamond ring. She started to cry and said yes. She hugged him."

I fear that I've run out of space, but will close by noting that Fred and Jamie did indeed tie the knot, with the wedding taking place in New York because "they both hated Tennessee." They honeymooned in Disneyland and Fred "feels like the luckiest man in the world."

I love happy endings, don't you?

Daily Courier, March 2009

SURPRISE PARTY HONORS 75.5 YEARS

Ric Hügo, an illustrator with the *Sacramento Bee* during my tenure there, came up with this sketch of me which, with one exception, is a very good likeness. The posture and girth, along with the sideburns and receding chin and hairline, are right on, but the nose is all out of whack. My nose doesn't protrude nearly as much as depicted. Incidentally, the unpublished sketch came about when a friend of Ric's asked him to come up with a caricature of his dentist and Ric was amenable but needed an idea as to what the dentist looked like in order to proceed. Well, the friend explained, "he looks just like Jerry Jackson." So Ric went on to do a bang-up job with the assignment, except for the nose. And despite Ric's commendable effort, the friend ended up huffing that the sketch didn't look anything at all like his dentist. That's gratitude for ya.

Yeah, that summertime birthday bash did indeed come as a surprise, especially in light of my having "discovered America" in December 1932. Wife Pat and daughter Shannon managed to pull it off by utilizing Shannon's e-mail address when extending invitations and responses. And during the gathering son Kerry recited a poem that he'd whipped up for the occasion, which read like so:

Back in Lubbock in late '32
A boy was born, and he grew and he grew
And grew some more till he was really quite tall,

So "Slats" he was called
By one and y'all.

Now it's not really his birthday,
But we can pretend,
And hope that you'll be able
To attend . . .
To raise a glass and holler "congrats"
And celebrate 75 years of Slats!

Surprise party honors 75.5 years (cont'd)

Now let it be said early on that Joanna and I both recognize raw talent when we see and hear it, and talent doesn't come any rawer than with The Stooges.

Yes, the reason behind that June 28 get-together at the Prescott home of Kim Robinson and Duff McGee came as a complete surprise. They're active in the Democratic party, see, so the scurrying around that wife Pat and daughter Shannon were doing in preparation for an alleged political gathering at their place that day fit perfectly. I'm a Democratic sympathizer, too, and did my part by cranking a freezer of ice cream for the event.

When I walked into the Kim/Duff backyard, though, a crowd of 70 or so friends and family greeted me for an unlikely birthday party. I say unlikely, since my birth date is Dec. 28! (The mood simply isn't conducive to such parties between Christmas and New Year's, see, so the bash was in recognition of my reaching 75 *and a half* years.)

And, hey, it was a warm and wonderful surprise. Shannon, via her personal email setup, mailings and phone calls, had dispatched the batch of invitations, and my niece, Jana Franklin, a Prescottonian, had been fielding various items that people had forwarded for display at the party. So the hush-hushiness going in was complete.

My sister, Shirley Hiser, and niece, Vanessa Goodwyn, had both flown in from Texas, and Shirley presented me with a beautiful pencil drawing she had done of my family and grandkids. Son Kerry drove over from San Diego and offered up some nice comments about ol' dad. A Prescott friend, Wayne Cramer, fashioned an attractive engraved plaque featuring a catchy birthday poem he had concocted. And a friend and neighbor, Kate St. Clair, sang a ditty to the tune of "Wouldn't It Be Loverly?" from "My Fair Lady" in which my church's choir director, Carole Nickerson, had penned the lyrics. A snippet: "We love you, Jerry, born in thirty-three/ Enjoy your life and your family/We wish you many more days, you see/Oh, Jerry, you're so elderly (oops, I mean *LOVERLY.*/Loverly. Loverly. Loverly. Loverly."

Birthday cards abounded, too. One showed a stork in flight, in the process of delivering a newborn babe, with this explanation: "Many years ago, a woman gave birth to a sweet, innocent bundle of joy." Then inside it asked: "What the hell happened?!" (If you guessed that someone other than Frank Finley passed that one along, then you're not a very good guesser.)

Then there was that musical birthday greeting from Courier reporter Joanna Dodder that featured The Three Stooges. Now, let it be said early on that Joanna and I both recognize raw talent when we see and hear it, and talent doesn't come any rawer than with The Stooges. The photo on the face of the card showed them behind a bass drum on which was written "The Original Two-man Quartet". Curly is playing a trombone, Moe is blaring on a trumpet, and the most versatile of the three, Larry, wields a drumstick in his right hand and a clarinet in his left. The music upon opening the card is their familiar "Listen to the Mockingbird" theme.

Speaking of quartets, The Grateful Four will be singing mainly gospel songs tomorrow at 6 p.m. at the Prescott United Methodist Church, 505 W. Gurley St., in conjunction with the church's "Wonderful Wednesday" program series. The four "half-pints" making up the "quart-et" include, alphabetically, Rod Bauer, Wayne Cramer, Sam Downing and Yours Truly. The gig is G-rated, too, as none of us will be uttering any cuss words during the entire program—I swear!—so feel free to bring along the kids if you like.

Prescott Courier, July 2008

HER NIGHTMARE'S ORIGIN BECAME
PAINFULLY CLEAR

"Beth approached him with a sterilized needle and medicine to lance the infection, but he would have none of it. He was more afraid of the needle than Imminent Death . . .and withdrew from the room, taking his thumb with him."
—Carol Hall

I have this sister-in-law, Albuquerquean Carol Hall, who couldn't make it to my surprise 75-and-a-half birthday bash that I elaborated on in a column last month. But she did send along a rundown to "Jerry's crowd" describing one of my quirks.

"Jerry is the eternal optimist; he will not give in to pessimism, so don't even try that around him," she wrote. "We've listened to him say 'Oh, no, I'm sure it will be all right' scores of times over the years, when we were convinced it would not be all right.

"The particular time I'm thinking of was when sister Beth and I were visiting Patsy and Jerry, and Jerry had a badly infected thumb and would NOT let anybody touch it. Beth approached him with a sterilized needle and medicine to lance the infection, but he would have none of it. He was more afraid of the needle than Imminent Death. 'Oh no, it'll be all right, it'll be all right, I'm sure! Naw, it'll be all right,' and he withdrew from the room, taking his thumb with him."

Unfortunately, the incident provided the catalyst for a dream–make that a nightmare–that night for Carol.

"I was sitting in Patsy and Jerry's house, but in a room I had never been in before," she recalled. "It was a rectangular room, very wide, but the other dimension was extremely narrow. The ceiling was two stories high, with a loft, which had a railing. I was seated on a bench on the wide wall, and the railing of the balcony was situated so that I had to tilt my head back to see the woman standing up there, holding on to the balcony. I have no idea who she was.

"To my horror, she suddenly pitched over the balcony, landing on her head directly in front of my feet, on the hard concrete floor! *SPLAT!* Aghast, I sprang up and bent over her to see if she was alive or dead. At that moment, Jerry strolled in with a bowl of ice cream he was eating. While kneeling beside the woman I told Jerry the story, while he looked down on the woman without concern, continuing with his chocolate-covered ice cream. Amazed by his indifference, I raised my voice and yelled 'Jerry, call 911! Call 911!' Jerry chewed a little more, and laughed a little small laugh and said, 'Oh no–I think it'll be all right, it'll be all right.'

"I woke up at just the moment I was looking up at him, helplessly–I guess my brain wasn't able to tack on a happy ending to that dream! The next day I realized where that dream came from!"

Such crassness on my part–even in a nightmare–is inexcusable. Maybe that ice cream was laced with marijuana and had dulled my senses. Anyway, I feel SO ASHAMED!

Prescott Courier, August 2008

Trying to "Comprende" Misplaced "A's" and "O's"

"El Pasa" would never work, nor would "La Paso". That would strip the masculinity from the name and make Marty Robbins turn over in his grave.

"At the foot of the jungle-covered Sierra Madre, overlooking the vast Pacific, Puerto Vallarta began life as a sleepy fishing hamlet. But after the 'Night of the Iguana' was filmed here in the 1960s, the whole world discovered this picture-perfect village. It was a slice of Old Mexico, where burros clattered down cobblestone streets and flame-hued bougainvillea spilled across white stucco walls."

That lead-in, coupled with some colorful photos and additional picturesque commentary, highlight a two-page spread in the current issue of *Texas Monthly*. Which is all well and good, except that I have a bone to pick with whoever named the town. You see, the Spanish language is fraught with feminine and masculine references, which traditionally have to agree with each other. So to be perfectly honest in its application, the name should be either Puerto Vallarto or, failing that, Puerta Vallarta.

This language quirk was drummed into my developing brain back at Lubbock High by my Spanish teacher, Mrs. Burford, who I think must've liked me more than a lot of the other kids because she signed my yearbook thusly: "Con amor a un gran alumno–Señora Burford." (Note that she called me an alumno instead of an alumna and that she had an "a" instead of an "o" at the end of her "señora" because she was a female lady.)

Now I know what you're thinking, which is that "puerto" is Spanish for "port" and that one shouldn't fool around with its spelling simply to accommodate an appendage ending in "a". But consider, if you will, the negative impact of getting fast and loose with, say, El Paso. "El Pasa" would never work, nor would "La Paso". That would strip the masculinity from the name and make Marty Robbins turn over in his grave.

So let's stick with the agreeableness inherent in such names as El Centro, La Canada and La Habra in California, Las Vegas in Nevada, Los Alamos in New Mexico, La Junta in Colorado and El Reno in Oklahoma, OK? After all, bisexuality in the naming of cities is tacky in my estimation. Thank you!

Meanwhile, I really hate to belabor the point at any more length, but feel compelled to take note of that sort of strange fellow, Don Quixote, who went around tilting at a bunch of windmills in Cervantes's classic "Man of La Mancha". This is not to say that many of the windmills didn't *DESERVE* being tilted at, but poor Don–who was skinny as a rail and rode around on that underfed nag of his–seemed to carry it to the extreme while simply refusing to listen to reason from his trusty manservant, Sancho Panza.

But back to the subject at hand, which relates to the Spanish language's affinity for femininity and masculinity as it applies to specific situations. You see, La Mancha (which may be a fictional town or even a state of mind) is pretty wimpy when mentioned in the same breath as that purveyor of willful backbone, Don Quixote. In fact, knowing Gov. Schwarzenegger as I do, it wouldn't surprise me at all to hear him call La Mancha a "girly town".

So my solution to the dilemma is to change the name of the book and stage play to make it much more macho, just like Don himself. "Man of El Mancho" would fit nicely, I think. And yes, I'm aware that such a change borders on an impossible dream because all you feminists out there (and you know who you are!) would never sit still for it. But you can't blame a fellow for tryin'.

Prescott Courier, December 2009

'O' OR 'A,' MALE OR FEMALE, I WAS KIDDING!

"So how would you like some foreigner trying to change the name of the city of Jackson to Ciudad Jacksona, just because ciudad is feminine?"
—Pancho Piñata

I tried to make last week's column both lyrical and satirical. I don't know about the former, but the latter fell like a lead balloon as far as a couple of website responders are concerned.

You see, I didn't–in my wildest dreams–think for one minute that anyone would take seriously my conundrum regarding masculine and feminine usages in the Spanish language, but it indeed happened.

If you're a good recaller, you may remember that I lapsed into some profound silliness regarding the "o" and "a" not agreeing as far as Puerto Vallarta goes (suggesting, with tongue embedded firmly in cheek, that a change to "Puerto Vallarto" might be in order), and that the Cervantes novel titled "Man of La Mancha" might fare better and give more heft to Don Quixote's macho image by changing "La Mancha" to "El Mancho". I was trying to be funny, but failed miserably in the eyes of a couple of readers.

There was this observation by Pancho Piñata:

"Misplaced? You should read the rules of the Real Academia Española. There are irregular genre words as well. Like mano (hand), that one would think is masculine, but it is actually feminine. And by the way, Vallarta is a last name, much like Prescott. So how would you like some foreigner trying to change the name of the city of Jackson to Ciudad Jacksona, just because ciudad is feminine? This article is pointless. Sure, an interesting little rant. And yes, irregular tenses and genres suck. English past tenses suck for non-native speakers."

(That really put me in my place, that's for sure! Actually, though, I think that "Jacksona" has a nice ring to it and carries with it a certain charm. It certainly flows better than, say, "Jackdaughter," eh? But enough of this silliness!)

And then there was this offering from someone labeling himself or herself as "An Informed Comment":

"Well, you know, that's the way it is. And Vallarta is a last name. Probably Ignacio Luis Vallarta is rolling in his grave for this article. A proper noun cannot be changed to fit the genre of the previous word."

(This is all very true, of course. And Google alerts me to the fact that Señor Vallarta was a Mexican jurist who fought in the Reform War on the side of Benito Juarez and later served as governor of the Mexican state of Jalisco from 1872 to 1876. His baptismal name was Jose Luis Miguel Ignacio Vallarta Ogazon, but that's probably more than you wanted to know. And if you're rolling in your

grave regarding that "Vallarto" reference, sir, then please know that I was only kidding and meant no disrespect.)

I did receive one positive e-mail in response to the column, though, which was heartening. Señora De Dolan had this to say on the subject: "As a follow-up to your Tuesday column, what do you think about the new name of Elderhostel? It is 'Exploritas' (explore + veritas). Obviously thought up by someone 'back east.' I immediately thought of 'little girl explorers' and I can't erase that image."

Thank you, lady! This allows me to boost my batting average in the Unrecognized Satire League to .333, which ain't all that bad, I suppose.

Prescott Courier, December 2009

NOW IF YOU SEE ME WITH A PURSE, I'LL EXPLAIN

Ruth used to whack poor ardent Arte real good, and I've got her technique down pat and will be able to respond in similar fashion.

It really did come as quite a surprise this past Thursday when I won the last raffle prize of the day awarded at the "Faces of AWEE" lunch & tea at the Prescott Resort. The main item in the bagful of goodies was a nice bejeweled purse. Yeah, you heard right.

AWEE, if you don't happen to be familiar with the acronym, stands for "Arizona Women's Education and Employment", so you're probably wondering what I was doing at the event in the first place. It's a legitimate question, since almost all of the attendees among the 200 or so souls there were women, and I'm not a woman. Never have been. Never will be.

Well, truth be known, I was there by invitation along with the other members of the singing trio I'm part of–Rod Bauer and Wayne Cramer–and our accompanying keyboardist, Chris Wuehrmann. We warbled some ditties ("Try to Remember", "Blue Skies", "You Raise Me Up" and "Goodnight, Sweetheart, Goodnight") as background music during the event and had an enjoyable time of it all.

But getting back to that special prize, which is my very first purse ever. The several raffle purses that went out each carried a theme, mine being "Cosmopolitan". It was donated by Rehab Boswell, a member of the AWEE Yavapai Advisory Council. (I wasn't familiar with that given name, but checked with her and learned that she was born in Amman, Jordan, and was named Rahab. However, she said, the name became Rehab when it was translated from Arabic to English.)

That "bejeweled" reference in the first paragraph has to do with the purse's exterior features, with "Cocktail Time!" being spelled out in faux diamonds (I suspect rhinestones). It is constructed of shiny reflective metal–sort of in the shape of a coffee can–and has a felt interior. Actually, it's quite classy and was one of several gifted items in the bag that also included bottles of cranberry cosmo and pomegranate martini mixes, a long-stemmed martini glass, a night light with paisley-plated stained glass (or maybe plastic), and handy items such as mascara, eye liner, lip gloss, eyebrow pencil and anti-wrinkle cream. For me, I'll admit, it represents a lifetime supply of such items.

Now, when I think of purses my first impulse is to recall Ruth Buzzi's weapon of first defense during those 140 riotous television episodes of "Laugh-In" that ran in the 1968-73 era. Upon Googling her website, I got a buzz out of a mention of Buzzi's role in that regard, which goes like so:

"Her most famous character is the dowdy spinster Gladys Ormphby, clad in drab brown with her bun hairdo covered by a visible hairnet knotted in the middle of her forehead. In most sketches, she used her lethal purse, with which she would flail away vigorously at anyone who incurred her wrath. On 'Laugh-In', Gladys most often appeared as the unwilling object of the advances of Arte Johnson's 'dirty old man' character Tyrone F. Horneigh."

So I'll here and now give fair warning to any guys who might make any sort of untoward comments if they spot me bopping around town carrying my purse. After all, Ruth used to whack poor ardent Arte real good, and I've got her technique down pat and will be able to respond in similar fashion. Consider this a warning and proceed at your own peril because I'm loaded with "purse-everance".

Prescott Courier, September 2010

POP ALONG THE ROW; I WONDER WHO, WHAT YOU'LL FIND

He was known as Judge Roy "The Law West of the Pecos" Bean, and many of the guys he sent to the gallows would've been better off remaining EAST of the Pecos because his motto was "hang 'em first, try 'em later."

Serendipity? Yeah. A healthy dose of it came my way on Dec. 12 when I trudged up to the nose-bleed section of the Yavapai College Performance Hall for a Prescott POPS Symphony concert.

I took my seat there on the back row of the balcony (great view!) and then what to my wondering eyes should appear in the seat to my right but Prescott's most beloved songbird, Toni Tennille! She was there with her sister, who she said is planning to move to Prescott too.

The sellout crowd was in for a major treat as the symphonics–under the capable wand of Paul Manz, originator of the POPS, who teamed up with guest conductors Darrell Rowader, Clydene Dechert, Richard Longfield and Joseph Place–staged a truly delightful and memorable Christmas concert. During the applause intervals, Toni–along with the throng of listeners–registered her approval with hearty "yips" and "yelps" reminiscent of same in a couple of her blockbuster hits–"Can't Stop Dancin'" and "Shop Around". Her enthusiasm was at fever pitch.

But let's revert to a quieter moment preceding the start of the concert when Toni mentioned that a friend had told her that a certain gift item she was seeking could be found at Trapper's Alley and asked me if I knew the location of the shop.

No, not really, I confessed, but replied that I *thought* that it was on Whiskey Row. Her next step was to fish out a hand-held computer, tap in "Trapper's Alley", and nailed down its location, which is indeed on the Row, huddling with the historic Palace Restaurant & Saloon.

A few days later, out of curiosity I dropped into the shop for a look-see and found an array of gift items including jewelry, clothing, baseball caps, key chains, coffee mugs and assorted knick-knacks such as those water-filled bulbs that produce snowfall when you shake 'em up.

But the most intriguing item I spotted was a T-shirt featuring a photograph proclaiming itself as "the most unique picture ever taken." It was shot in 1883 in Hunters Hot Springs, Mont., and included 15 men who were notables of one sort or another in that era. Guys like Wyatt Earp, Teddy Roosevelt, Doc Holliday, Bat Masterson, Butch Cassidy *and* the Sundance Kid, Judge Roy Bean and, among others, a fellow I never heard of but liked the sound of his name–one "Liver Eating" Johnson.

Space won't allow elaboration on but one notable, though, and that would be Judge Bean. Actually, I found out by Googling that his full name was Phantly Roy Bean Jr., and I can't really fault him for going with "Roy" instead of Phantly. A bit of background on him, though, reveals that he was a "hanging judge" who held court sessions in his saloon in Langtry, Texas, there on the banks of the Rio Grande. (Langtry, now a ghost town, got its name from Judge Bean himself. The "love of his life," you see, was British actress Lily Langtry—a woman he never met but someone he really had "the hots" for.)

Anyway, he was known as Judge Roy "The Law West of the Pecos" Bean, and many of the guys he sent to the gallows would've been better off remaining *east* of the Pecos because his motto allegedly was "hang 'em first, try 'em later." He was no doubt a legend among the putting-the-cart-before-the-horse crowd.

Prescott Courier, December 2010

Composer Choplin peppers Prescott with charm

Pepper, you see, salted his harmony hominy with just the right flavoring to leave a wonderful taste in one's mouth.

Pepper Choplin

In years past, I remember a regular feature in the Reader's Digest focusing on one's "most unforgettable character". Well, in my case that person surfaced this past weekend when he paid a visit to the Prescott United Methodist Church.

The name of this incredibly talented composer, vocalist, instrumentalist and humorist is Pepper Choplin. He hails from a Baptist church in Raleigh, N.C., which is fine because we're all brothers and sisters under the skin, with the only major difference being that they "wet wash" while we Methodists "dry-clean".

Anyway, he headed up three services–one on Saturday evening and two on Sunday morning–all of which were characterized by upliftedness and loving-kindedness. He's one of those humans harboring a hefty hunk of humaneness, and I just wish that the world could be Peppered with more Choplins. Were that the case, I guarantee that it would be a much better world.

Pepper, you see, salted his harmony hominy with just the right flavoring to leave a wonderful taste in one's mouth. He provided some serious fun at the Saturday service, too, which featured two PUMC choirs along with a choir from the Unity Church of Prescott and a busload of choristers from Glendale in the Valley. All in all, some 140-plus voices contributed to the program, singing individual Choplin selections, and they also combined as a mass choir to present a finale featuring four of his compositions.

One segment of the program related to Pepper's account of what happened when his dog happened to eat his Holy Bible, rendering it "more holey." He recounted the story with evangelistic zeal. What occurred is a "Rover's Digest" that prompted a spate of indigestion upon poor Rover, who suffered the predictable aftermath. Quite a spiritual ritual, I must say, as Pepper sprinkled his commentary with take-offs on the names of various books in the Bible. 'Twas an ever-lovin' hoot.

From a sort of related standpoint, I received an e-mail last week from one Richard Kimball (aka Old Man Coyote), who forwarded a list of items that have actually appeared in church bulletins or been announced in church services. (As an aside, Richard's wife, Vicki, was the accompanist for the Choplin piece that the Unity Church group sang on Saturday.)

Two of the items are ones that everyone armed with a computer has no doubt picked up from the e-mail circuit, but they have to do with choirs, so bear repeating. One stated that "next Thursday will be tryouts for the choir. They need all the help they can get." The other: "At the evening service tonight, the sermon topic will be 'What Is Hell?' Come early and listen to our choir practice."

I had previously heard many of the bulletin bloopers (for example, "The sermon this morning: 'Jesus Walks on the Water'. The sermon tonight: 'Searching for Jesus'." But several were new to me, and here's the cream of the crop:

- "The pastor would appreciate it if the ladies of the congregation would lend him their electric girdles for the pancake breakfast next Sunday."
- "The church will host an evening of fine dining, super entertainment and gracious hostility."
- "Potluck supper Sunday at 5:00 p.m.–prayer and medication to follow."
- "This evening at 7 p.m. there will be a hymn singing in the park across from the church. Bring a blanket and come prepared to sin."
- "Remember in prayer the many who are sick of our community. Smile at someone who is hard to love. Say 'Hell' to someone who doesn't care much about you."

Yeah, it's hellish to relish a church in the lurch. (Just thought I would end this little treatise with some poetic nonsense. The passage just sort of burst forth, so please accept my apology.)

Prescott Courier, March 2011

REUNION TRIP SHOWS WHAT A SMALL WORLD WE LIVE IN

Bill helped us along by pointing out that "La Quinta" translates to "next door to Denny's" in Spanish.

Say, that was a super senior citizen soiree that surfaced last week down there on the Texas coast. The event was the 14th annual Road Buddy reunion, which this year took place in Galveston, with the participating parties being old friends from Texas Tech and also Lubbock High School, all 10 of whom have been married to each other in the neighborhood of 50 years, plus or minus. If "marriage is bliss," then you might say that we're just a bunch of "bliss-ters".

Leading the longevity pack with 57 years together were Orville and Claire Summey of North Richland Hills, a Fort Worth suburb (Orville's a retired architect); James and Beth Sides of Lafayette, La., at 56 years (James scored both touchdowns back in '51 when Lubbock High beat Baytown 14-12 for the state championship and was the starting fullback for Texas Tech when it downed Auburn 35-13 in the 1954 Gator Bowl. During his playing career from 1953 to 1955 at Tech, he had a still-standing record of 6.2 yards per carry, lost only 3 yards and never lost a fumble during his career, and in August 2011 was inducted into the university's Athletic Hall of Fame); Bill and Sharlene Gaither of Richardson, a Dallas suburb, at 54 years (Bill's not the gospel songwriter of the same name, but rather a guy who grew up to become an oral surgeon); wife Pat and I of Prescott, at 49 years (I'm a retired newspaper bum); and Leon and Jeanne Taylor of Fort Worth, at 47 years (Leon is a retired accountant with Bell Helicopter).

We all headquartered at a La Quinta motel on Seawall Boulevard (Bill helped us along by pointing out that "La Quinta" translates to "next door to Denny's" in Spanish, and that held true when it came to our Seawall digs). As was the case with much of Galveston, the motel was hit hard by Hurricane Ike in September 2008. Its ground-level floor was flooded, and the renovation took a year before the place could be reopened.

Anyway, we all had a fine time doing such things as visiting the Lone Star Flight Museum housing vintage and latter-day aircraft; hopping the Bolivar ferry ("the greatest free ride in Texas"); enjoying some fine dining that included a dandy dinner of seafood succulence at the 100-year-old Gaido's restaurant; and checking out some of the grand old homes on the

Artist Dale Lewis created this majestic heron that rose like a phoenix from the stump of a Hurricane Ike-obliterated Oak on Ball Street in Galveston.

island, many of which featured elaborate carvings fashioned from the stumps of olden oaks that Ike took out in its fury.

The most unusual occurrence of the get-together, though, took place while the 10 of us were batting the breeze in the lobby area of our motel. Nothing too heavy, of course. In fact, James, Beth and I were reminiscing about our time at Lubbock High. For example, there was a mention of Bill "Toe" Davis, who came by his nickname honestly due to his being the punting specialist for the LHS Westerners. (The guy could be counted on to kick the ball out of bounds inside the 10-yard line with regularity.) Well, Beth mistakenly referred to Toe as "Moe", though, which is understandable because the team in that era did indeed have a "Moe"–Morris "Moe" Turner–but he was a quarterback who never got into punting. He was a class of '50 grad who would go on to serve as Lubbock's mayor in 1972-74. (As an aside, Beth was a '54 grad–one year ahead of classmate Buddy Holly.)

Moving right along, there was a certain amount of hilarity and guffawing going on when a fellow approached our happy group and commented that he enjoyed "listening to stories" and asked if he could join in on the listening, and we of course welcomed him. Well, after identifying himself as Greg Brummet, the inevitable "where ya from?" question came up and he replied that he was from Richardson. Since Bill and Sharlene hail from the same city, Bill asked him what part of town he lived in, and they both expressed a mutual awareness of their mutual whereabouts. Then when Bill provided him with his own full name, the fellow interjected something quite unexpected.

"Hey," he said, "you pulled my wisdom teeth back in 1969!" Then he gleefully extracted his cell phone and called his wife to let her know of the chance meeting with the guy who extracted his chompers 42 years ago.

Yes, this is indeed a small world in which we live.

Prescott Courier, April 2011

Thoughts on Texas' secession and a doleful Dalmatian

Pat and Dalmatian

Now frankly, I doubt that the five-way split will ever take place because Texas is still hankering to become No. 1 in size again once Alaska thaws out.

As wife Pat and I were driving from Prescott to Galveston earlier this month on Interstate 10, we stumbled across one of those green-and-white "official" highway signs that struck us as strange. After spending the night in Las Cruces, N.M., we were motoring along just a few miles out of El Paso at the time, with the distance being duly noted on the sign, but just below that bit of information was the reference to: "Beaumont 852".

Now, I-10 snakes through such major cities as San Antonio and Houston before reaching Beaumont (just west of the Louisiana line) and terminates in Jacksonville, Fla., where the Atlantic Ocean gets in the way. So what's with the reference to Beaumont? At the risk of over-dramatizing, I would hasten to call it one of the mysteries of our time.

There were some other catchy references on billboards and the like along the way. The familiar "Drive Friendly" signs in Texas were complemented by one that urged: "Eat jerky. Don't drive like one". And a law firm's billboard suggesting infighting by proclaiming that "we sue lawyers". And near San Antonio was a sign advising that we were about to cross "Woman Hollering Creek". Another small roadside sign asked voters to cast ballots for Gale Pospisil for mayor of New Braunfels. (Pat and I flipped out over the possible pronunciation of that surname and would never try saying it fast, three times in a row.) There was a sign on a Galveston restaurant noting that it's "where the elite meet in bare feet". And, to top it off, we spotted an imposing billboard near Galveston, complete with website, with this angry suggestion: "Yes, we *CAN* secede!".

In the latter regard, though, it's my impression that secession isn't a valid concession without a lot of aggression which even Texas couldn't successfully pull off without a lot of help from a bunch of other sympathetic Southern states. And I seriously doubt that those other states would be all that interested in the enterprise anyway. Now, there's a provision in the constitution of the Republic of Texas (the only state in the Union that was a republic before it was annexed in 1845) that Uncle Sam went along with stating that it could be split into as many as five states by a vote of its people, but secession wasn't mentioned in the document. Now frankly, I doubt that the five-way split will ever take place because Texas is still hankering to become No. 1 in size again once Alaska thaws out.

But enough of this insipid speculation because I need to take note of some more Galveston sculpturing before I run out of allotted space. Last week's column focused on a beautiful heron that artist Dayle Lewis carved out of the stump of an oak tree that Hurricane Ike took out in September 2008. The accompanying photo features not one but two other sculptures that another artist, Jim Phillips, carved from tree stumps. They are located on the grounds of Galveston's City Hall, near Fire Station 1, and reek with poignancy. A dalmatian, you see, is seated on the lawn and is gazing longingly at the sculptured likeness of a fireplug about 20 yards away.

It's seldom that companion sculptures can tell a more touching story.

Prescott Courier, April 2011

A Heartfelt Farewell to Dear Ol' Nick & Doris

Nick Davirro

"He was awesome and we are going to miss him. I know he's hitting on the ladies in heaven right now."
—Claudine Callaway

At 130 pounds, Nick Davirro was a lightweight as an amateur boxer, but a heavyweight in all other aspects of life. He lived it to the fullest, spreading levity and lightheartedness among all those with whom he came in contact. He was, in a word, a "hoot".

My first contact with Nick and his lovely wife, Doris, came about in 2007 when they made up 50 percent of a bowling team of which I was a participant, and we've been competing in a league at Prescott's Plaza Bowl ever since. Sadly, though, fate stepped in last Tuesday when they were fatally injured in a traffic accident when the driver of an oncoming pickup truck swerved over the double yellow line and struck their SUV head-on at Chino Valley's south town limits. Nick was 91 or 92, whereas Doris was 81.

I say "91 or 92" advisedly because the news account of the crash listed him as 91, but I've written about Nick in the past, attended the last couple or three of his December birthday bashes, and feel comfortable with that 92 figure despite the accusation of a mutual friend of Nick's and mine, Frank Finley, that Nick was prone to exaggeration. Be that as it may, there is no question as to Nick's nonagenarian-ness.

(It was Finley, incidentally, who fashioned a commemorative trophy last year for Nick after he bowled a 192 line. It's 3 and ¾ inches tall and, as I noted in a subsequent column, "is displayed as prominently as possible on Nick's mantle in his Chino Valley home.")

It must be noted that Nick's bowling prowess was on occasion erratic. In fact, I remember one time when he got a strike, which of course earned him total pins on his next two rolls, both of which were gutter balls. But that's not as bad as it sounds, in that one throw was in the east gutter and the other settled in the west one, so it reflected excellent balance on Nick's part.

Nick's antagonist in the bowling league has always been Skip Hansen, and the two of them would lay down wagers every week while taking into account Hansen's enhanced ongoing average. And they pretty much broke even over the years, according to Skip. (As an aside, Skip said that Nick was active in another area of wagering and that he and Doris would motor over to the Safeway on White Spar Road on a weekly basis and hop a bus to Camp Verde's Cliff Castle Casino for some gaming, and that Nick swore up and down that he "*always* won." Skip went on to add, though, that he accompanied them on one such occasion and that Nick lost big-time. It wasn't Nick's fault though, as he confided to Skip that the loss occurred because "they had taken out his favorite machine." Those casino people should be ashamed of themselves, I say.)

Nick, it must be said, led a varied life. He was a U.S. Marine during World War II, and there's a book titled "The War: An Intimate History 1941-1945" that contains a photo of him on those terrible sands of Iwo Jima. All of his fellow Marines are hugging the terra firma as they inch up the slope, but the inimitable Nick is up on his haunches, looking much like a prairie dog, while smiling for the camera. Among his other pursuits he also worked as a miner and did a lot of cowboying in the area valleys of Williamson and Skull.

The tribute wouldn't be complete, though, without a timely testimonial submitted to me by a granddaughter of his, Claudine Callaway of Phoenix. "He loved Prescott and the people of Prescott and Chino," she wrote, "and "I know he would have lived to be 100 had this (the accident) not happened. He would tell anyone why he believed that, too," she added, because of some healthy advice that "a spoonful of Vaseline a day keeps you 'lubed up' inside. He would also tell me to go to bed late and wake up early" and to "have a few tablespoons of olive oil a day as well." Also, he advised against "getting one of those handicapped signs that you hang on your mirror when you can walk! I remember him arguing with my mother because she had one," telling her that 'I don't need that garbage; I can walk from Prescott to Chino just fine!'

"He was awesome and we are going to miss him. I know he's hitting on the ladies in heaven right now."

Yeah, heavenly ladies, be on your guard, 'cause ol' Nick is on the loose!

Prescott Courier, June 2011